YORK PERSONAL TUTORS

Handling Data

Cassandra Lee

YORK PERSONAL TUTORS

titles in series

GCSE English

Novels and Short Stories
Shakespeare
Film and Media
Poetry
Drama
Spelling, Grammar and Punctuation

GCSE Maths

Number Book 1
Number Book 2
Shapes, Space and Measures
Algebra
Handling Data

YORK PRESS
322 Old Brompton Road, London SW5 9JH

PEARSON EDUCATION LIMITED
Edinburgh Gate, Harlow
Essex CM20 2JE, United Kingdom
Associated companies, branches and representatives throughout the world

© Librairie du Liban *Publishers* and Pearson Education Limited 2000

First published 2000

ISBN 0582 42467 4

Page layout and diagrams by Cauldron Design, Berwickshire, Scotland
Illustrated by Spike Gerrell
Film output by Spectrum Colour
Printed in Malaysia, KVP

CONTENTS

Introduction   4

H1 Collecting Data   6

H2 Hypotheses and Questionnaires   12

H3 Simple Graphs   16

H4 Frequency Distributions, Histograms and Frequency Polygons   19

H5 Pie Charts   25

H6 Conversion Graphs   30

H7 Scatter Graphs   33

H8 Averages   38

H9 Averages from Grouped Data   43

H10 Cumulative Frequency   48

H11 Histograms   57

H12 Standard Deviation   62

H13 Simple Probability   70

H14 Estimating Probability using Relative Frequency   76

H15 Listing all Outcomes   79

H16 Mutually Exclusive Events   83

H17 Finding the Probability of Combined Events   87

H18 Conditional Probability   93

Index   96

Introduction

This Personal Tutor is all about Data Handling. You may have bought this book because you want to develop your skills in this area, or boost your GCSE grade.

This book is in two sections. The first section shows you how to solve real-life problems by encouraging you to think about what information needs to be collected, how it should be collected, and how it should be presented in order to make sense of it.

The ability to handle statistical information (data) is an essential skill. You can see data presented in different ways all around you, in the newspapers, on TV, on billboards, and on the Internet. Companies use data-handling skills to produce advertising campaigns for new products to make them appear even more fantastic. Governments present information about the country to persuade people that they are doing a good job (sometimes in misleading ways!). Medicine manufacturers have a huge impact on how we treat some of the world's most devastating diseases through the results of their research into new medicines.

The second section teaches you how to calculate how likely an event is to happen, and whether a game or raffle is worth playing, through Probability Theory.

THINK ABOUT IT

Would you like to win the lottery? We all know that it is extremely unlikely to happen, but do you know exactly how unlikely?

The probability of winning is 1 in 13,983,816.

Can you see how this was calculated?
Read sections ▶ H13 onwards!

This book will not magically improve your chances of winning, but it will help you to estimate whether it is really worth playing!

This book contains a lot of references to the Personal Tutor Number Books 1 and 2. This is because you will need a good grasp of the topics in these books to help you understand some of the techniques involved in Data Handling, especially for the section on Probability. You will also need good estimation skills to help you decide if your answer seems sensible.

There are three possible ways of using this book to help you through your exams:

1. You can work through the book from start to finish, chapter by chapter. The book has been set out in a logical sequence to make this possible.

2. If there are particular topics you want to focus on or revise, you can look up just that chapter, or series of chapters which deal with that area. This is especially useful if you want to revise a topic you are studying at school.

3. The Key Concepts give you concise pieces of information that you need to know for a particular topic – particularly useful for rapid revision just before the exam.

Throughout this Personal Tutor Handling Data Book, the emphasis is on helping you build up an understanding of why things work and how they can be applied to everyday life, rather than a series of methods to be learnt in isolation. We hope that this book, and the others in the series, will help you to improve your Maths and get an excellent result at GCSE, but most of all that you ENJOY working your way through it.

H1	Collecting Data	H1

When you do a survey, you need to record the data that you collect in some way. If there are only a few pieces of data, you could just write a list.

Companies collect data to see if their products are attractive. This is called market research. For example, Scoff It chocolate manufacturers asked five people which colour wrapper they preferred on their latest chocolate bar.

The replies were: red, blue, red, green, yellow.

This doesn't tell me very much about which colour is the best, because there isn't enough data. The company needs to ask hundreds of people to get a better idea, but if they write all these people down in a list it would be very long and difficult to understand.

Here are the replies for the first twenty people:

> red, blue, green, yellow, red, yellow, red,
> blue, red, yellow, yellow, blue, red, red,
> green, blue, green, red, yellow, red

They record the replies in a **tally chart**, as follows:

Colour of wrapper	Tally	Frequency
Red	||||| |||	8
Blue	||||	4
Green	|||	3
Yellow	|||||	5

Every time someone says they like red, the company researcher will tally one mark in the row for red. When they get to five people saying red, they put a line through the previous four marks. This makes it easier to count up large totals after the survey is completed.

The final column is the total number of tallies. This is called the frequency.

This shows that red is the most popular colour wrapper, so far.

 Collecting numerical data

This works in the same way. For example, another company asked its workers how many chocolate bars they eat every week.

The replies were: 3, 2, 4, 0, 1, 6, 25, 0, 2, 5, 1, 1, 2, 5, 12, 2, 4, 2, 1, 7.

Draw up a tally chart showing the number of chocolate bars chosen. The smallest number of bars is 0 and the largest is 25. The tally chart must cover all these options.

A tally chart which lists all the numbers from 0 to 25 would be very large. Let's group together all the numbers that are 'more than 7'.

Number of chocolate bars eaten	Tally	Frequency
0	II	2
1	IIII	4
2	HHt	5
3	I	1
4	II	2
5	II	2
6	I	1
7	I	1
more than 7	II	2

The most common number of chocolate bars eaten is two.
Five people ate two chocolate bars in the week.

Collecting data in groups

We can create tally charts for discrete numerical data. In the previous section each tally chart had a row for each single data value. The only chart which didn't was the chart showing the number of chocolate bars. This was because a tally chart showing every data value from 0 up to 25 chocolate bars would have been very long.

In this case, we grouped together all the people who said they ate more than seven chocolate bars in one group. This technique is very important when you have a large number of data values.

For example, suppose you collected data on the times taken by twenty people in an egg and spoon race, and the times, in seconds, are as follows:

| 10 | 21 | 12 | 27 | 24 | 15 | 13 | 11 | 14 | 17 |
| 21 | 24 | 14 | 21 | 24 | 23 | 12 | 23 | 16 | 20 |

The shortest time is 10 seconds and the longest is 27 seconds. A tally chart covering every data value from 10 to 27 would be very long.

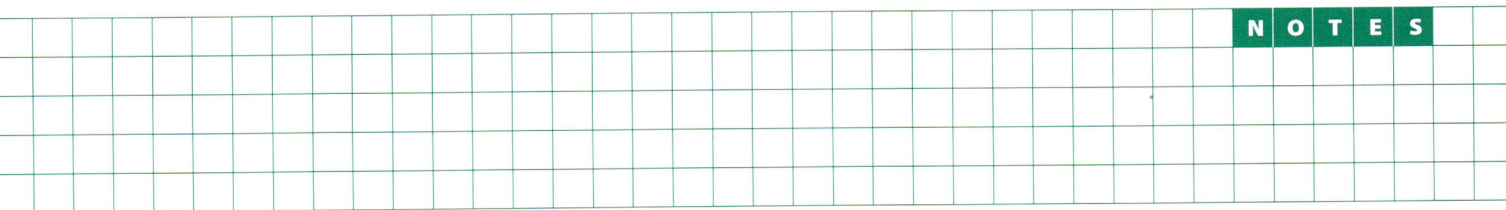

NOTES

We need to group the values together. Groups of five seconds would be a good idea.

The first group would be: **10 to 15 seconds**

The second group could be: **15 to 20 seconds**

If we had to tally the time of 15 seconds we wouldn't know which group to tally it in, because it appears in both groups.

Let's think again.

The first group should be: **10 to 14 seconds**

The second group would then be: **15 to 19 seconds**

It's now clear that a time of 15 seconds would be tallied in the second group.

Let's set up and complete the tally chart.

10	21	12	27	24	15	13	11	14	17
21	24	14	21	24	23	12	23	16	20

The first data value is 10.
It goes in the group 10–14.

The second value is 21.
It goes in the group 20–24.

Times (seconds)	Tally	Frequency
10–14	卌 II	7
15–19	III	3
20–24	卌 IIII	9
25–29	I	1

THINK ABOUT IT

Why do you think there are **two** large groups for this egg and spoon race?
Maybe the second group of people dropped their eggs and had to run back!

✳ Recording continuous data

There are two types of numerical data.
Discrete data are data that take only whole number values.

Examples of discrete data are:
- Number of brothers and sisters
- Number of chocolate bars eaten
- Times in a race if they are measured to the nearest whole number of seconds
- Marks out of 10 given in a competition

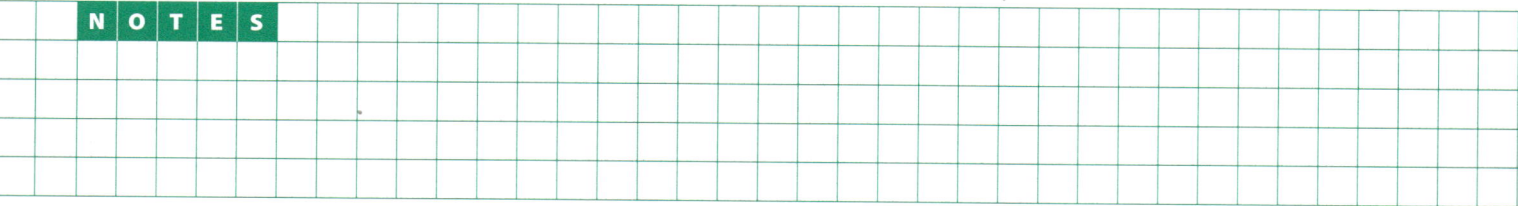

N O T E S

Continuous data take every value in between. This means the data could have decimal values.

Examples of continuous data are:

- Measurements. For example, height can take every value. It cannot be measured exactly, but only to the nearest centimetre, or even millimetre. The accuracy of the measurement depends on the accuracy of the measuring instrument.
- Age. Most of the time we say we are a certain number of years old. If we are more accurate we could say we are a certain number of years and months old. Even more accurately we could talk about days, hours, minutes or even seconds.

Most continuous data are actually treated as discrete data, because they are rounded to the nearest whole number when measured.

EXAMPLE   Bill is doing a survey to find out whether the shelves in the library are the right height. He measures how far up the wall twenty-five people can reach, in metres.

He recorded the following results:

1.81	2.40	2.09	2.10	1.98
2.15	2.36	2.19	1.87	2.03
2.14	2.24	2.56	2.01	2.23
2.31	2.07	1.93	2.18	2.30
2.16	1.95	2.27	2.39	2.22

To choose the groups, first look for the smallest and the largest data values. The groups must go between these two values. The smallest value is 1.81 and the largest is 2.56.

There is no fixed rule about how many groups you should have, but between five and ten is about right.

We need to go from 1.80 up to 2.60. This is a gap of 80 centimetres. Eight groups of 10 centimetres would be simplest.

The first group is written as **1.80 and up to but not including 1.90**. This allows us to plot data values that are measured as **very close** to 1.90 but not **quite** there.

We **could** have written 1.80–1.89 for this group, and then 1.90–1.99 for the next group. Strictly speaking this is wrong as there would be no way of recording a value between 1.89 and 1.90 (for example 1 metre, $89\frac{1}{2}$ centimetres). As measurement is continuous we may have to record a length like this.

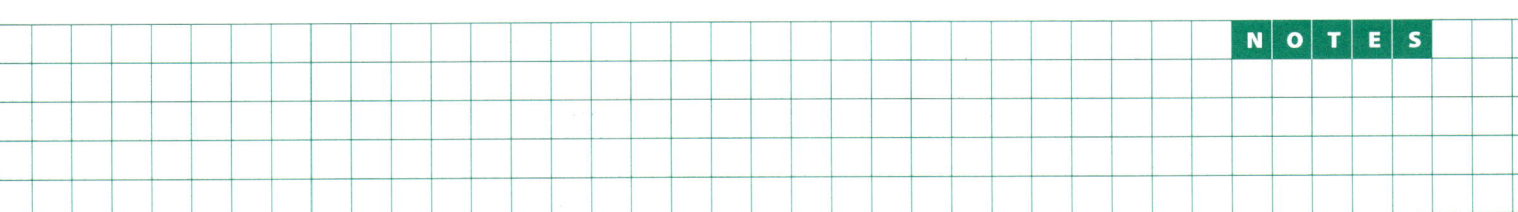

The first data value is 1.81 and is tallied in the group **1.80 and up to but not including 1.90**.
The second data value is 2.40 and is tallied in the group **2.40 and up to but not including 2.50**.

Continuous data groups may be written as inequalities. If reach height is written as h, then the group **1.80 and up to but not including 1.90** may be written as:

$$1.80 \leq h < 1.90$$

This means that h is greater than or equal to 1.80 m but strictly less than 1.90 m.

For everyone to be able to reach the top shelf it would have to be 1.80 metres high and no higher.

Reach height (m)	Tally	Frequency
$1.80 \leq h < 1.90$	II	2
$1.90 \leq h < 2.00$	III	3
$2.00 \leq h < 2.10$	IIII	4
$2.10 \leq h < 2.20$	IIII I	6
$2.20 \leq h < 2.30$	IIII	4
$2.30 \leq h < 2.40$	IIII	4
$2.40 \leq h < 2.50$	I	1
$2.50 \leq h < 2.60$	I	1

THINK ABOUT IT

How high would **you** make the shelves?
You need to think about whether you make them the height that **most** people can reach, or the height that **all** people can reach. Perhaps we need to talk about the **average** reach height. You can find out more about that in sections ▶ H8, Averages and ▶ H9, Averages from Grouped Data.

KEY CONCEPTS

✳ Tallying up data in groups makes it easier when your data take a large number of values

✳ Choose your groups (**class intervals**) so that they are all the same size, and the size is an easy number

✳ Find the gap between the largest and the smallest value. Divide this by the number of groups you want to get the group size. You should have five to ten groups

✳ If the data are discrete (whole number values) label the groups so no value occurs in more than one group. For example, ages in groups of 10 years might be 0—9, 10—19, 20—29, and so on

✳ If the data are continuous label your groups so that the data values can go right up to the highest value in each group. For example, 0 cm and up to 5 cm, 5 cm and up to 10 cm, and so on

✳ Continuous data groups may be written as inequalities. For example, $5 \leq l < 10$ means that l is greater than or equal to 5 but strictly less than 10

NOTES

REVIEW

1. Twenty-five people training for the London–Brighton bike ride were asked how far they had cycled yesterday.
   The distances in kilometres were:

9	15	42	31	27
49	18	16	22	32
12	19	13	48	14
36	4	18	20	6
23	30	26	8	34

   Copy and complete this tally chart for these data.

Distance (km)	Tally	Frequency
0–9		
10–19		
20–29		
30–39		
40–49		

2. One morning, people coming out of a supermarket were asked several questions in a survey. One of the questions was 'How much did you spend?' Here are the amounts collected:

£24	£18 .42	£60 .13
£29	£34 .67	£40
£40 .02	£32 .34	£37 .13
£33 .23	£59 .99	£28 .14
£57	£30 .98	£38
£48 .54	£25	£38 .23
£45	£34	£28 .67
£41	£29 .01	£20

Amount spent	Tally	Frequency
	Total	

   a. Choose your **own sensible group intervals** for the amounts collected.
      Hint! Choose something similar **£0 and up to £20** for your first group.

   b. Use your group intervals to copy and fill in the tally chart above.

Answers

1.

Distance (km)	Tally	Frequency
0–9	IIII	4
10–19	HHT III	8
20–29	HHT	5
30–39	HHT	5
40–49	III	3

2.

Amount spent	Tally	Frequency
£0 and up to £20	I	1
£20 and up to £40	HHT HHT HHT	15
£40 and up to £60	HHT II	7
£60 and up to £80	I	1
	Total	24

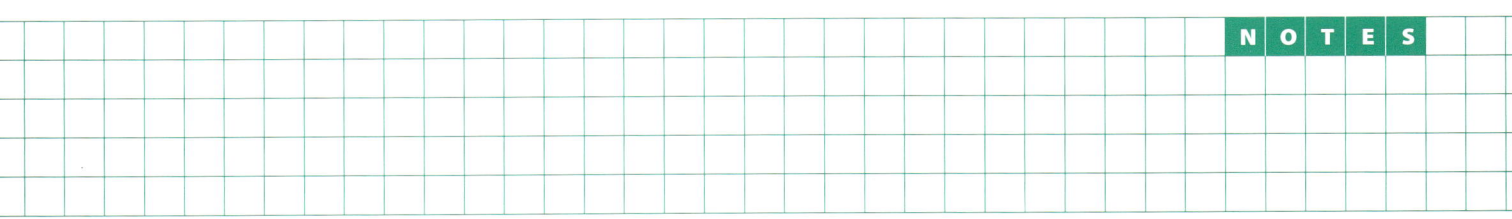

H2 | Hypotheses and Questionnaires | H2

When you choose to do a survey you need to ask yourself one very important question. **Is the survey worth doing?**

This may seem like a silly question, but there is no point in collecting data just for the sake of it. You must be trying to find out something as a result.

You need to be quite specific about what you are looking for. It is no good saying you will do a traffic survey, for example. Ask yourself what it is about the traffic you are looking for. You then need to set yourself a hypothesis.

✳ Hypothesis testing

Whenever you do a survey, you should try to set yourself a hypothesis. A hypothesis is a theory that may or may not be true. You test your hypothesis by collecting relevant data.

Examples of types of surveys and some possible hypotheses are:

Type of survey	Possible hypotheses to test
Traffic surveys	• Red cars go faster than cars of other colours • Women drive faster than men • Most cars break the speed limit
People surveys	• Boys eat more chocolate than girls • The taller you are the longer your toes are
School or work-based surveys	• Most children dislike doing homework • Maths is everyone's favourite subject • People work longer hours in offices than in shops • Small animals sleep less • Big animals eat more • Dogs are the commonest pet
Leisure interests	• Most people watch at least 10 hours of television every week • The more television you watch the cleverer you are • Violence in films encourages violence in real life • The more goals scored by a football team, the more points gained in the league table
World surveys	• The poorer a family, the larger the family size • The greenhouse effect causes global warming

NOTES

12

Some of these hypotheses may be true and some may not be. Some of them are easy to test and some need specialised data collection.

You need to know how to design a survey to test your hypothesis once you have decided what it is. Issues you need to take into account are:

- What data you need to collect?
- How are you going to collect them?
- Where are you going to collect them and from whom?
- How are you going to record them?
- How are you going to display your results so that you can prove or disprove your hypothesis?

When you are tackling these questions, you need to keep your hypothesis in mind all the time. Let's take some of the hypotheses above in turn.

Red cars go faster

You need to collect speeds of a range of cars of different colours. You could then find out what the average speed is for each colour (see ● H8, Averages). You can then conclude whether red cars are fastest, or whether another colour is faster.

The taller you are the longer your toes are

You will need to measure people's heights and their toe lengths. You must make sure you collect data from a wide range of people (different ages, different sexes, and so on). You must make sure you are measuring in the same way each time. You could then plot a scatter graph (see ● H7, Scatter Graphs) of height against toe length. Your graph should show some form of link between the two groups of data.

Most people watch at least 10 hours of television every week

Collect data on how often people watch television. Your recording sheet could give a range of different times for people to choose. For example, you could ask them how many hours they watch in a week. They could choose from: 0 to 9 hours or 10 or more hours.

Make sure you ask a wide variety of people.

Calculate what proportion of the people watch at least 10 hours per week. If it is more than half of the people surveyed then your hypothesis is true.

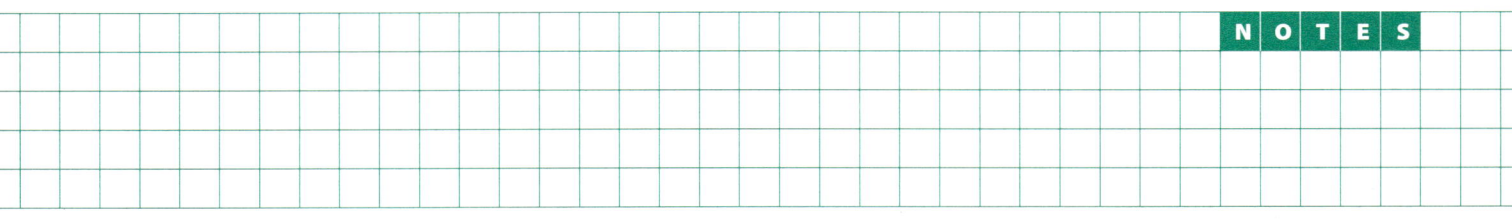

N O T E S

❋ Questionnaires

When you want to collect a lot of different information about people, you can design a questionnaire. You can record the answers or you could let the person you are questioning record them.

Whatever you choose, bear in mind the following points when writing the questions.

Be very clear about what you want to find out

Make the question very specific. For example, *'Do you like television?'* is not specific enough. You are likely to get answers that are difficult to record. Are you asking how much television they watch, or whether they think television is a good thing?

A clearer request would be:

Record how many hours you watch television on the table below:

0 to 4 hours	5 to 9 hours	11 to 14 hours	15 to 19 hours	20 to 24 hours

You may want to find out if children enjoy doing homework. *'Do you enjoy doing homework?'* is too vague, and is probably going to get a negative reaction! A better way to find out is: *Tick one of the boxes opposite to describe how you feel about homework.*

I enjoy doing homework	
I enjoy some of the homework that I do	
I dislike doing homework	
I have no opinion	

Don't ask questions that are likely to offend people or which may encourage a certain response

Here are some bad questions:

- Do you use deodorant?
- Most healthy people don't eat chips. How often do you eat chips?

NOTES

Ask a variety of people, of different ages and sexes, and at different times of the day and in different places

This is called getting a **quality sample**

Here are some bad places to do surveys that will probably lead to biased results:

- *What is your favourite football team?*
  If you stood outside Manchester United's football ground on a Saturday afternoon, you would get very different results than if you stood in the centre of Liverpool.

- *Most healthy people don't eat chips. How often do you eat chips?*
  Imagine asking this inside a fast food restaurant. Not only would you get biased results, but you would also upset the people you were asking, and the management of the restaurant!

KEY CONCEPTS

When doing a survey, what specifically are you trying to find out? ✳

Set up a hypothesis that you are going to test ✳

Collect data that are relevant to the question. Be clear about what you are asking ✳

Do not make questions too vague, biased towards a certain opinion or offensive ✳

Ask a variety of different people ✳

And remember, is your survey worth doing? ✳

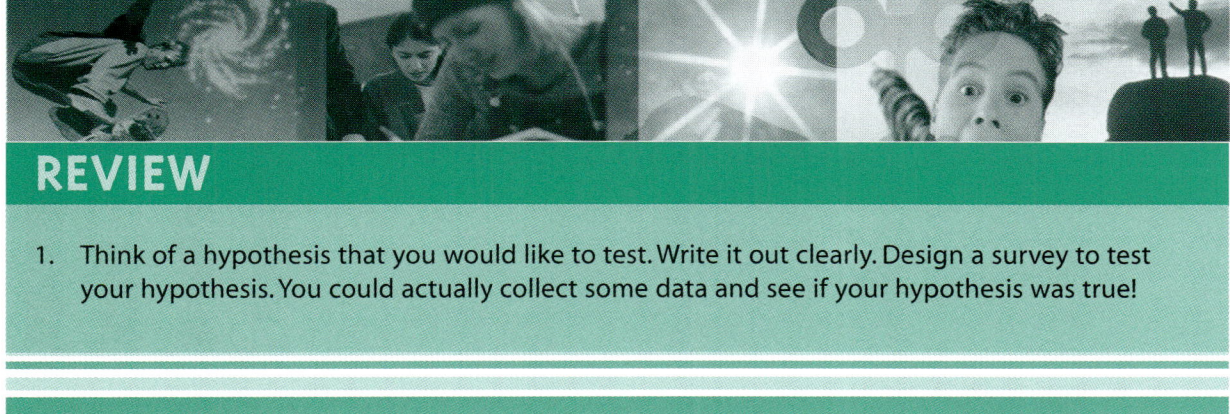

REVIEW

1. Think of a hypothesis that you would like to test. Write it out clearly. Design a survey to test your hypothesis. You could actually collect some data and see if your hypothesis was true!

| H3 | Simple Graphs | H3 |

When you do a survey, and you have recorded the data in a chart, you need to draw some conclusions. Sometimes you can just look at the data and make certain conclusions quite easily. It is even easier to see trends and to draw conclusions if the data are displayed in some form of graph.

Graphs help you to see the most or least common item, and show comparisons between sets of data in a more obvious way.

In this section we will look at some basic graphs and how to draw them.

Bar charts

A bar chart helps you to see the most and the least common item in an obvious way. A bar is drawn for each data item and the height of the bar represents the frequency (amount) of that data item.

In ● H1, Collecting Data, we looked at people's choice of colour for the wrapper round a bar of chocolate.

The results are shown opposite.

Colour of wrapper	Frequency
Red	8
Blue	4
Green	3
Yellow	5

The chart shows clearly that red is the most popular colour wrapper.

A bar chart would help us to make comparisons between the choices in a more obvious way.

The colours of the wrappers (these are the data items) are listed along the horizontal axis. The frequency is listed up the vertical axis. Each square represents one person's choice. All the bars are the same width and there is a gap between each bar. They are equally spaced.

The axes are clearly labelled and the graph has a title describing what it shows.

The chart shows that twice as many people preferred red to blue. We can see this clearly because the bar for red is twice the height of the bar for blue.

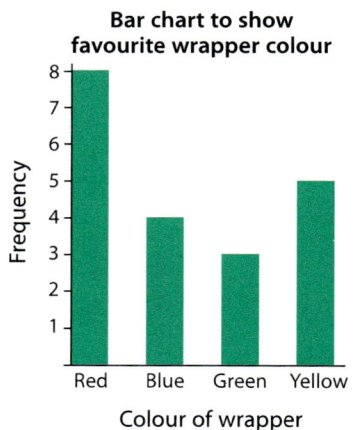

Bar chart to show favourite wrapper colour

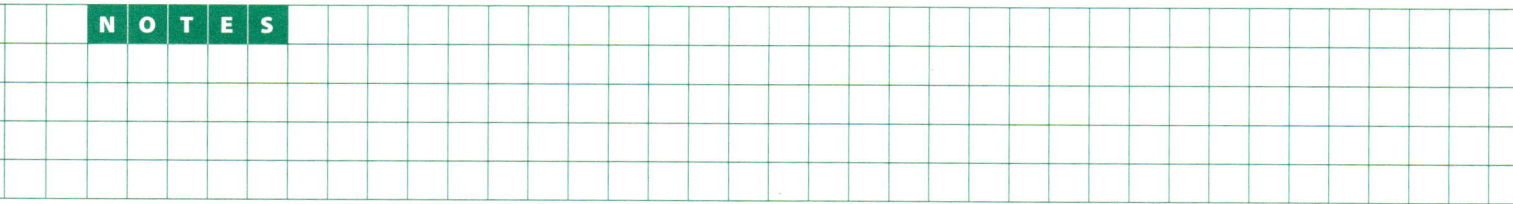

✳ Pictograms

A pictogram is a pictorial bar chart. Instead of drawing bars, we draw a picture to represent each item.

You could use one picture for each person's choice. If the number of items is large you can choose to use one picture to represent more than one person's choice. If you do this it is important to do a key to say how many people one picture represents.

The pictures must be equally spaced out and the same size, so that the length of the 'bar' of pictures is proportional to the frequency it represents. If you draw the pictures different sizes, you could end up with bars of the same frequency being of different lengths. This is misleading. For this reason, it is important to choose a simple picture which is easy to repeat exactly.

EXAMPLE A leading sweet manufacturer asked twenty teenagers which type of chewing gum they preferred. Their answers are shown in this chart:

Type of chewing gum	Frequency
Squidge	6
Jaw-ache	4
Chew Haloo	7
Wrigglees	3

I want to draw a pictogram, using one chewing gum symbol to represent two people. This means I need to draw three symbols for Squidge because 6 ÷ 2 = 3. I need to draw $3\frac{1}{2}$ symbols for Chew Haloo because 7 ÷ 2 = $3\frac{1}{2}$.

Note that the symbols are all the same sizes and are equally spaced, so that the length of the 'bar' for Wrigglees is exactly half the length of the bar for Squidge.

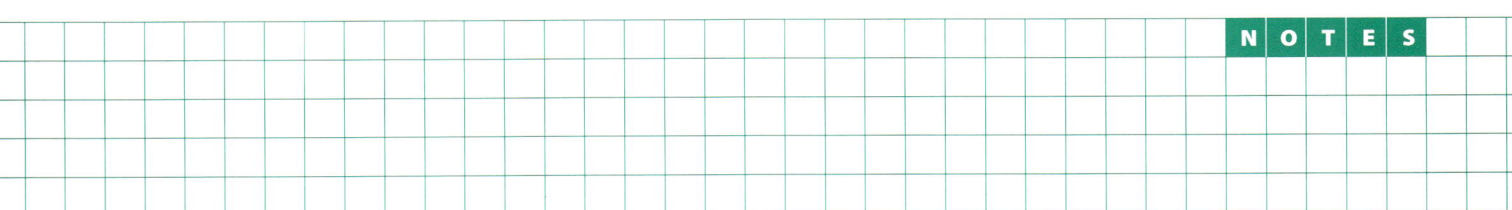

Chewing gum choices

Key

represents two people

KEY CONCEPTS

❋ Bar charts show the frequency of each data item as the length of the bar

❋ Pictograms show the frequency by the number of symbols

❋ For all graphs: label axes clearly with the description of the data item; do a title describing what the graph shows; and if drawing a pictogram, do a key to show how many items each symbol represents

REVIEW

1. The chart shows the winnings paid out from a game at a fair.

   a. Draw a bar chart of the data.

   b. Draw a pictogram of the data. Remember to do a key.

   c. Which type of graph did you find the easiest and why?

Winnings	Frequency
0p	56
5p	24
10p	17
50p	3

Answers

1. a. Bar chart to show winnings of people at a fair

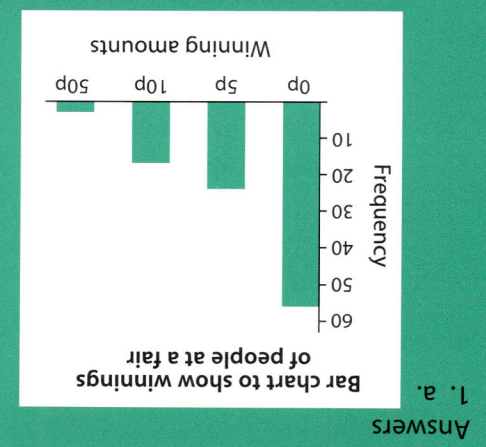

b. Pictogram to show winnings of people at a fair

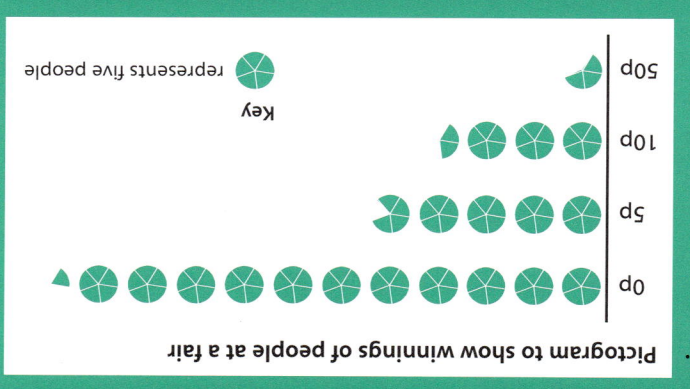

c. For a small number of data items like this (only four items) a bar chart probably shows the data in the clearest way.

For high frequencies a pictogram can be confusing to draw and to read values from, but it does look pretty!

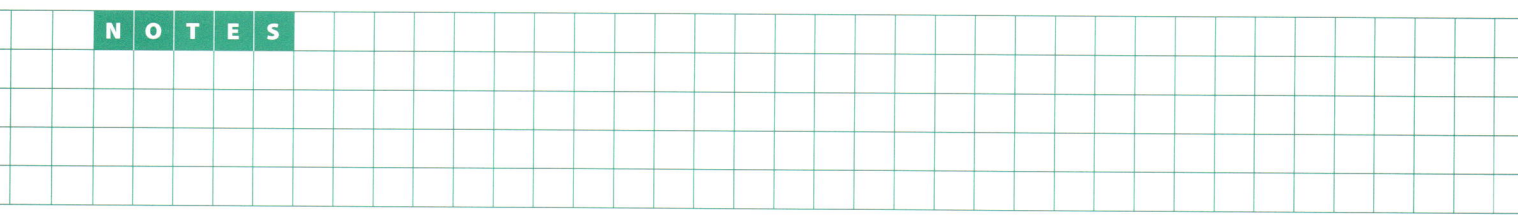

H4 | Frequency Distributions, Histograms and Frequency Polygons | H4

In ○ H1, Collecting Data, we created tally charts for grouped data. We need to be able to draw graphs of data in groups. We also need to be able to compare two or more sets of data using their graphs.

 ## Histograms for continuous data

A histogram is a special form of bar chart.

For grouped data, the data lie between two limits. The bar is therefore drawn between these two limits.

In ○ H1, Collecting Data, we met Bill, who was doing a survey to find out whether the shelves in the library are the right height. He collected the data in this tally chart:

Reach height (m)	Tally	Frequency
$1.80 \leq h < 1.90$	II	2
$1.90 \leq h < 2.00$	III	3
$2.00 \leq h < 2.10$	IIII	4
$2.10 \leq h < 2.20$	HHT I	6
$2.20 \leq h < 2.30$	IIII	4
$2.30 \leq h < 2.40$	IIII	4
$2.40 \leq h < 2.50$	I	1
$2.50 \leq h < 2.60$	I	1

The groups go in blocks of 0.1 metres, so the horizontal axis should run in steps of 0.1. The first bar runs from 1.80 m to 1.90 m. It is drawn two units high.

The histogram looks like this:

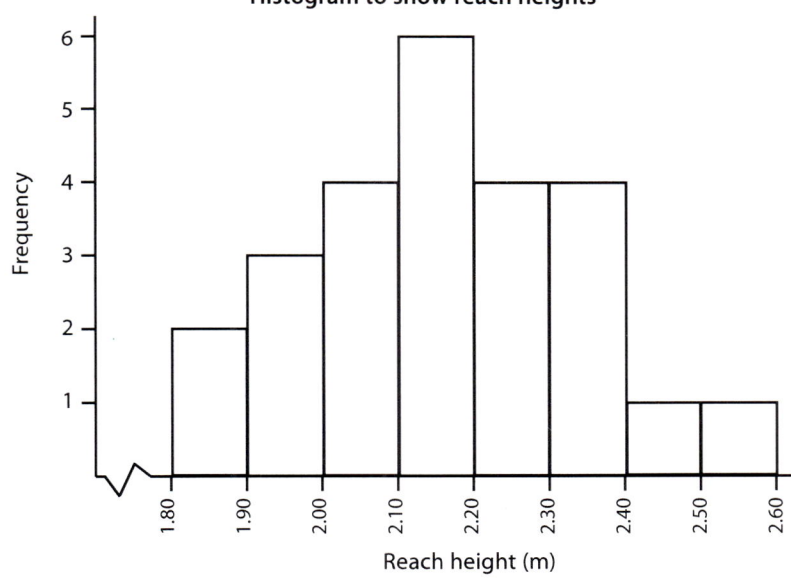

Histogram to show reach heights

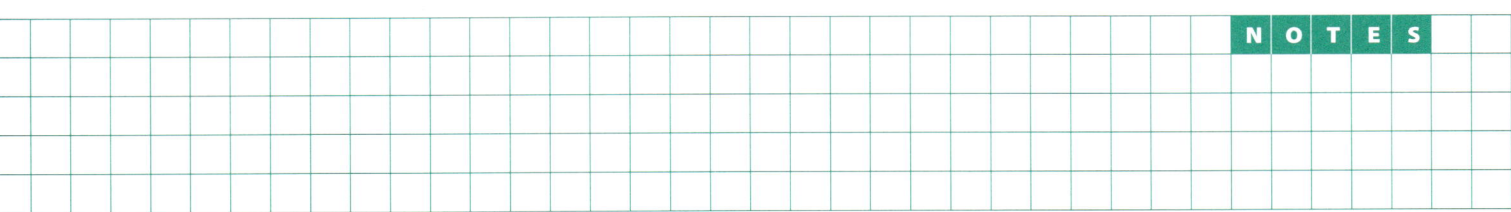

Histograms for discrete data

Here are the data again about the times taken by twenty people in an egg and spoon race. The times are given correct to the nearest second.

Times (seconds)	Tally	Frequency
10–14	卌 II	7
15–19	III	3
20–24	卌 IIII	9
25–29	I	1

The data in the table are *discrete* because they have been rounded to the nearest second. Time is actually a *continuous* variable.

This means that the first group actually lies between 9.5 seconds and 14.5 seconds.
The second group runs from 14.5 seconds up to 19.5 seconds.
We can now plot the histogram without any gaps between the bars.
The horizontal axis becomes a continuous scale.
The first bar is drawn between 9.5 seconds and 14.5 seconds.

The graph looks like this:

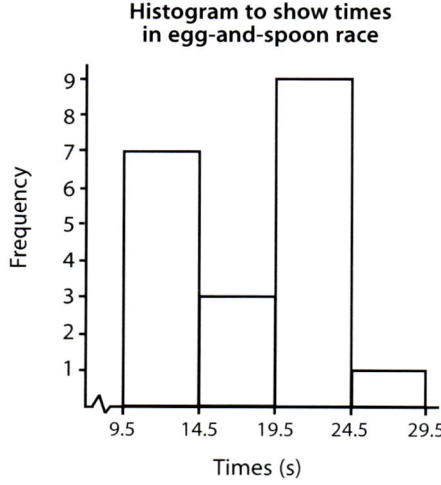

Histogram to show times in egg-and-spoon race

The shape of the graph is interesting.
It shows two peaks. Two groups have high scores. Why do you think this is?

Frequency Polygons

Frequency polygons are line graphs adapted to fit grouped data.

Look back at the histogram for the first example.

I plot a single point in the middle of each bar at the top.

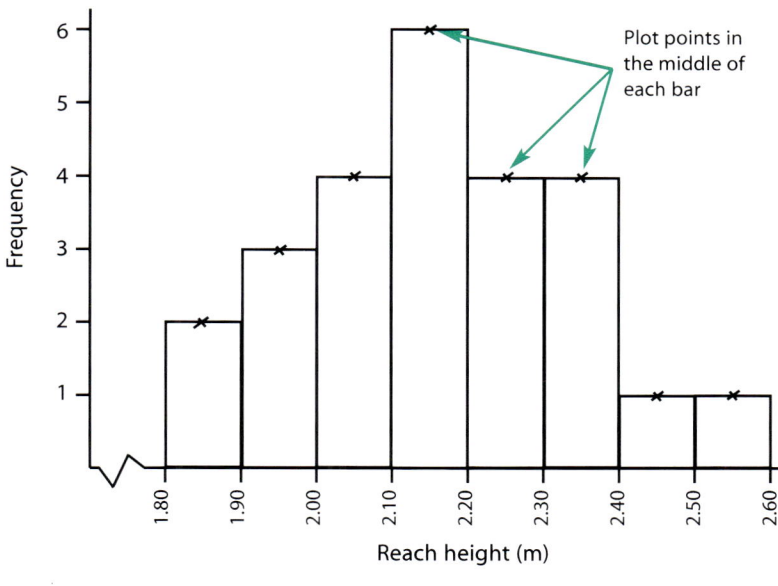

Histogram to show reach heights

Plot points in the middle of each bar

If the bars are now rubbed out, and the points joined up with straight lines, the result is a completed frequency polygon. Without the bars it looks like this:

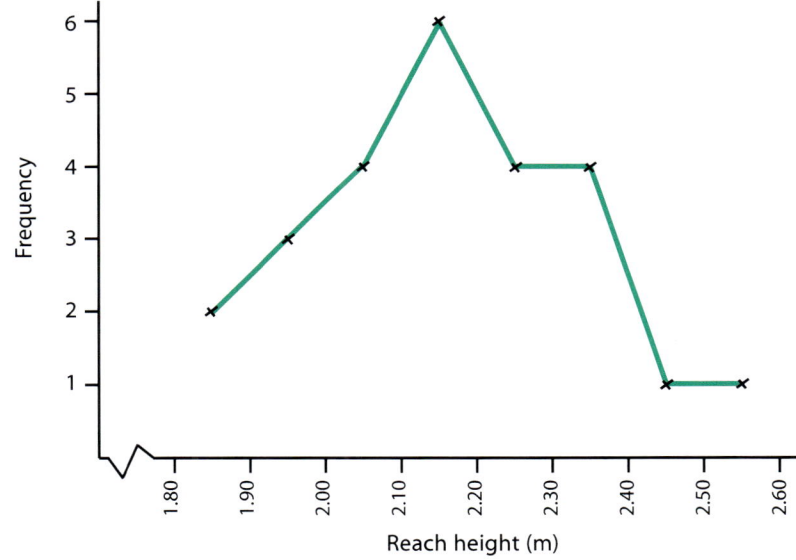

Frequency polygon to show reach heights

One advantage of a frequency polygon is that it is quicker to plot than a histogram. You don't need to plot the bars first. Just plot the points.

You can also plot two graphs on the same axes, which enables you to compare two groups of data very easily, as the following example shows.

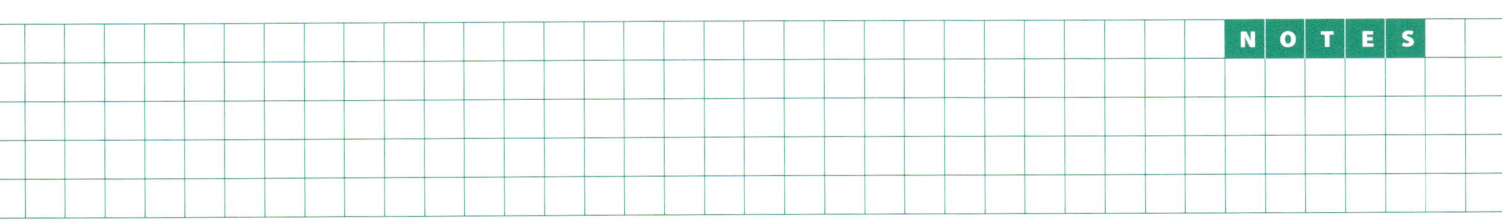

EXAMPLE

The frequency polygon of the egg and spoon race data given on page 20, is drawn here.

I want to compare the performance of these athletes with the performance of the athletes at the Olympic egg and spoon race. The data for the Olympics are given here:

Times (seconds)	Frequency
10–14	10
15–19	5
20–24	4
25–29	1

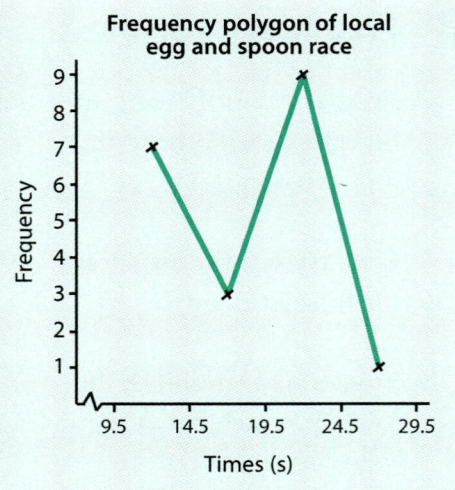

Frequency polygon of local egg and spoon race

I can plot a frequency polygon of this data on the same axes as the first graph.

It is now easy to compare the distribution of times of the two races.

In the first race, the times peak twice and in the second they only peak once. Perhaps this is because fewer people in the Olympic egg and spoon race have to run back for their egg!

The Olympic graph peaks sharply at times 10–14 seconds. This shows that more of the Olympic athletes finish faster.

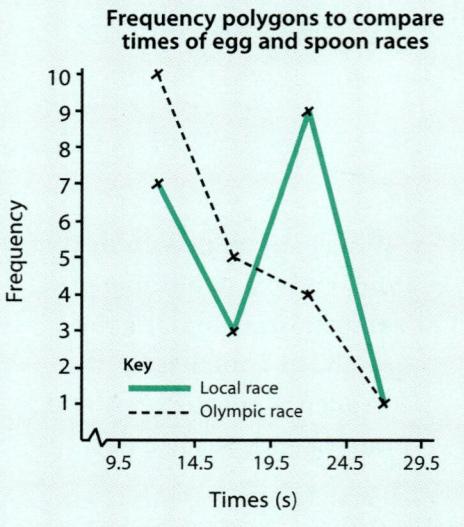

Frequency polygons to compare times of egg and spoon races

Key
— Local race
---- Olympic race

KEY CONCEPTS

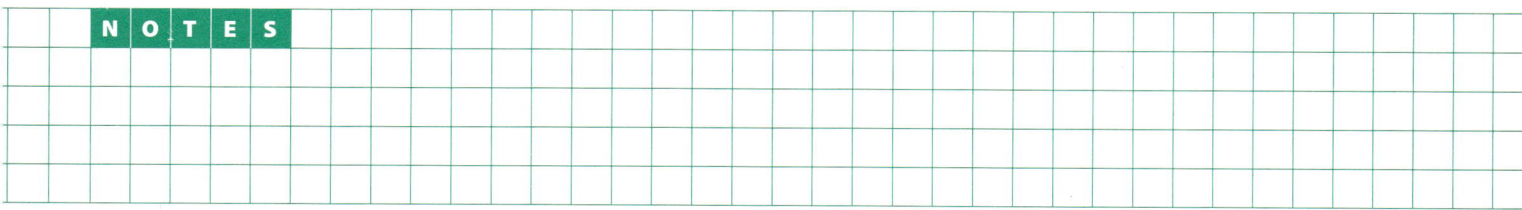

❋ A histogram or a frequency polygon is used to graph data in groups

❋ Both graphs have a continuous horizontal scale with no gaps between groups

❋ For a histogram, the bars lie between the two limits of the group

❋ If data are given as discrete but are actually continuous, plot the bar half a unit wider on either side to make the scale continuous

❋ For a frequency polygon, plot a single point in the middle of the group, then join the points up with straight lines

❋ A frequency polygon is usually used to compare two sets of data on the same graph

N O T E S																			

REVIEW

1. Twenty-five people training for the London to Brighton bike ride were asked how far they had cycled yesterday. The distances, given to the nearest kilometre, were:

Distance (km)	Tally	Frequency
10–19	卌 II	7
20–29	卌 IIII	9
30–39	卌 I	6
40–49	III	3

Plot a histogram of these data. Be careful! The data are actually continuous, so you need to make the horizontal scale continuous (like the egg and spoon race example).

HIGHER PERFORMANCE

1. The data below show the hours worked by the twenty-five employees at Shopper's Paradise.

Hours worked	Tally	Frequency
$0 \le h < 10$	卌 卌 卌 II	17
$10 \le h < 20$	卌	5
$20 \le h < 30$	II	2
$30 \le h < 40$	I	1

An identical survey was done at Legal Beagles, a firm of solicitors.

Hours worked	Tally	Frequency
$0 \le h < 10$	I	1
$10 \le h < 20$	II	2
$20 \le h < 30$	IIII	4
$30 \le h < 40$	卌 III	8
$40 \le h < 50$	卌 IIII	9

Draw two frequency polygons on the same axes to compare the spread of hours worked in the two companies. State two differences between the distributions. Explain these differences.

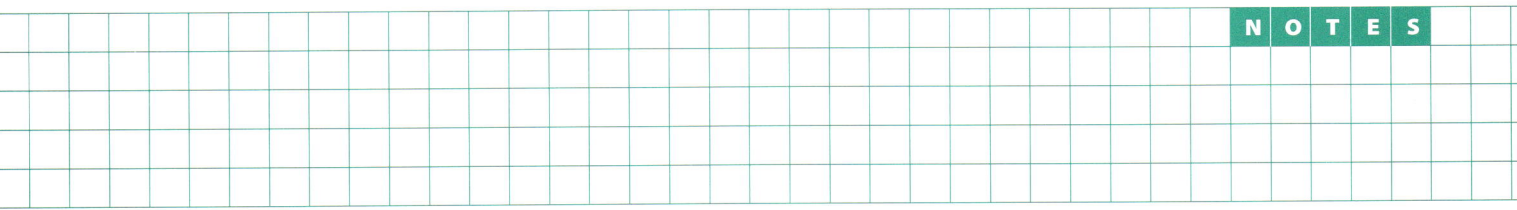

Answers

1.

Frequency polygons to compare hours worked

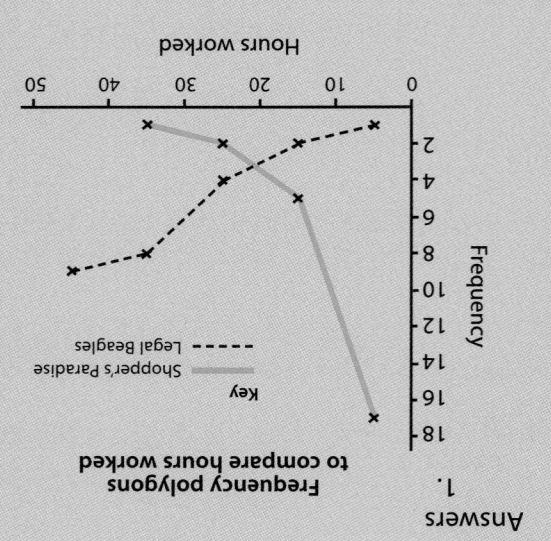

Some comparisons are as follows:

- The range of hours worked is greater for Legal Beagles. (The graph goes from 0 to 50 hours, which is a range of 50. The graph for Shopper's Paradise goes from 0 to 40 hours, which is a range of 40.)

- On the whole, people work longer hours in Legal Beagles (the graph for them peaks at a higher number of hours). There are far more part-time workers who work fewer hours at Shopper's Paradise. The number of hours worked is slightly more evenly distributed across the Legal Beagles graph. (The Shopper's Paradise graph peaks sharply at the group 0 to 10 hours, whereas the graph is flatter for Legal Beagles.)

Answers

1.

Histogram to show distances cycled

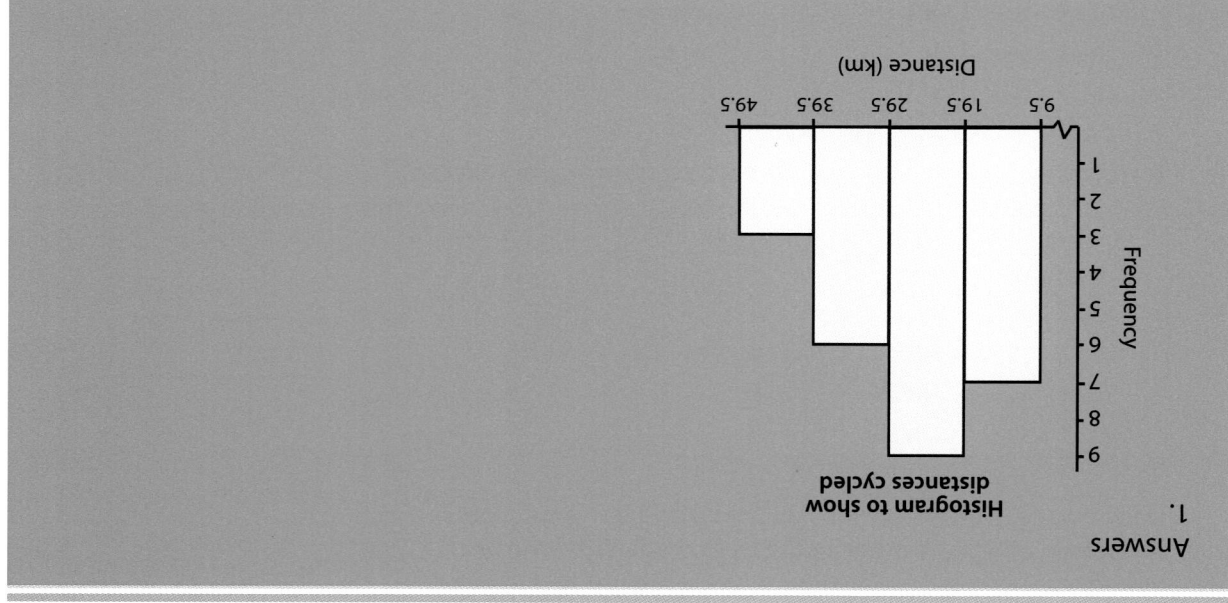

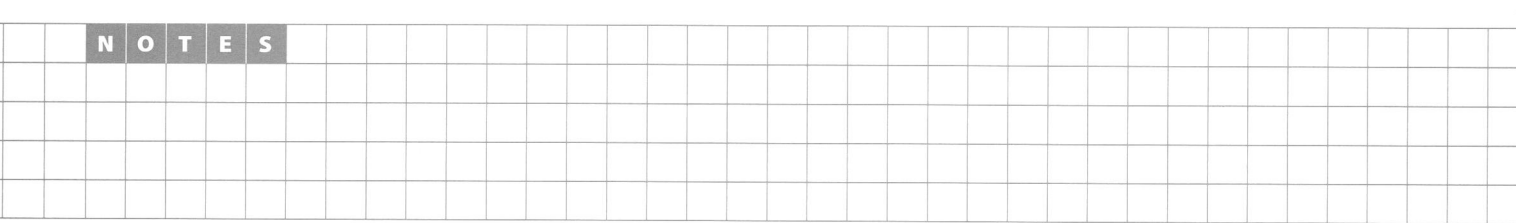

H5

Pie Charts

H5

A pie chart shows the proportions (see ▶ N15, Basic Proportion/Ratio) of each item as a slice of a pie. It is used to show how something is divided up between different items.

A slice is called a **sector** of the pie chart.

Most pie chart questions can be estimated using proportion methods.

The pie chart opposite shows how a pupil spends one whole day. The day is divided up into different activities.

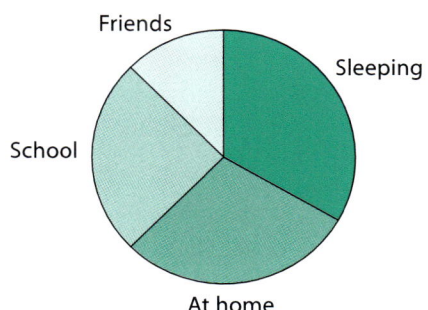

We need to decide how much of each day is spent on each activity. A day is 24 hours.

The sector spent at school is 90°. This is $\frac{90}{360} = \frac{1}{4}$ of the pie chart.
To find a quarter $\left(\frac{1}{4}\right)$ divide by 4. Pete spent 24 ÷ 4 = 6 hours at school.

The sector for friends is half the size of the sector for school.
This means he spent three hours with friends (6 ÷ 2 = 3).

The sector for sleeping is $\frac{120}{360} = \frac{1}{3}$ of the pie chart.
He spent 24 ÷ 3 = 8 hours asleep.

The last sector represents all the rest of the day.
This is 24 − (6 + 3 + 8) = 7 hours at home doing other things.

The method used simple fractions to work out the proportions given to each sector. The method can be applied in the same way when the fractions are not quite as simple, as the next example shows.

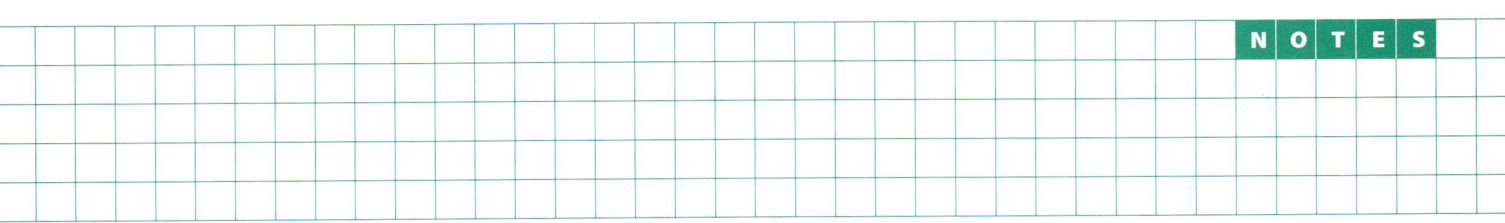

N O T E S

EXAMPLE

The pie chart shows how many votes were gained during the local elections. The total number of voters was 80 thousand. This has been divided up between different political parties.

Calculate how many votes were gained by each party.

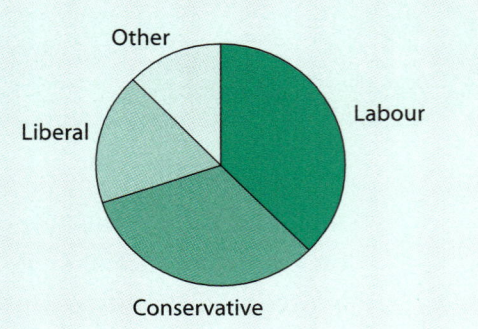

First measure the angles in the pie chart. It is important to be very accurate.

We have:

Labour	135°	Liberal	63°
Conservative	117°	Other	45°

In a pie chart there are 360°.
The fraction of the pie chart that is represented by Labour votes is $\frac{135}{360}$.

This is a bit more than $\frac{1}{3}$.

The number of people who voted Labour is therefore:

$\frac{135}{360}$ × 80 thousand = 30 thousand, which is a bit more than a third $\left(\frac{1}{3}\right)$ of the voters.

The number of people who voted Conservative is:

$\frac{117}{360}$ × 80 thousand = 26 thousand, which is a bit less than a third $\left(\frac{1}{3}\right)$ of the voters.

The number of people who voted Liberal is:

$\frac{63}{360}$ × 80 thousand = 14 thousand

The Others sector is easy. It is all the remaining voters.

The number of people who voted for other parties is therefore:

80 − (30 + 26 + 14) = 10 thousand

This is an eighth $\left(\frac{1}{8}\right)$ of the voters.
We know this is correct because 45° is an eighth $\left(\frac{1}{8}\right)$ of the pie chart.

N O T E S

✳ Drawing pie charts

The proportion of the pie chart that you give to each sector depends on two things:

- How many people in total are you representing on the chart?
- How many people are you representing in that particular sector?

A pie chart is always 360° all round.

Imagine we had just one person to represent on the pie chart.
That person would be represented by the whole pie chart; all 360°.

If we had two people they would each have 360° ÷ 2 = 180°.
That's half of the chart each.

Three people would have 360° ÷ 3 = 120°, or a third ($\frac{1}{3}$) of the chart each.

This pattern will continue until you have the formula:

angle given to each person = 360° ÷ total number of people on the pie chart

EXAMPLE

The following table shows how the pupils in one class get to school.

Display the information in a pie chart.
First calculate the angle given to each person.
There are twenty-four people altogether.
The angle given to each person is 360° ÷ 24 = 15°.

Transport	Frequency
Bus	10
Car	7
Walk	4
Cycle	3

The sizes of the individual sectors now depend on how many people are in each sector.

Ten people travel by bus, so we should have ten lots of 15°.

angle = 10 × 15° = 150°

Seven people travel by car: angle = 7 × 15° = 105°
Four people walk: angle = 4 × 15° = 60°
Three people cycle: angle = 3 × 15° = 45°

Always check that your angles add up to 360°.
Here 150° + 105° + 60° + 45° = 360°.

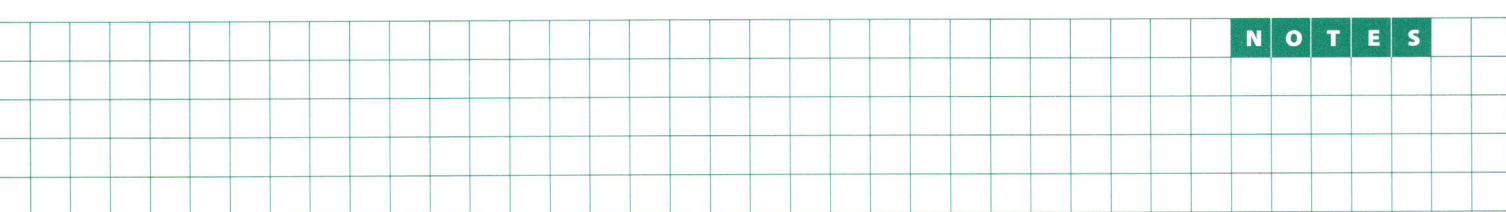

N O T E S

Now draw the pie chart.

Draw a circle with a radius of about 3 cm. The size is not important, but try not to make it too small.

Draw in one radius (a straight line from the centre to the outside). Draw the first sector from this. It should be 150° for the 'Bus' sector. Draw in all the other sectors in turn, and label each one with the name.

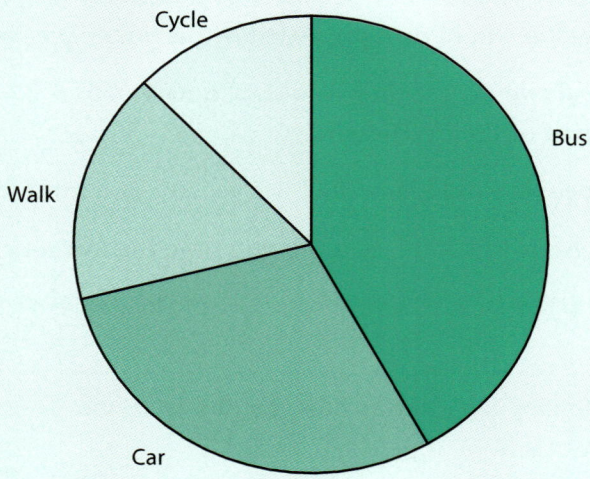

Note: It is usual to draw the largest sector first, followed by the others in order of decreasing size, finishing with the smallest.

KEY CONCEPTS

* A pie chart shows the frequency of each data item as the size of the sector of the pie

* To get rough numbers from a pie chart, look at the fraction of the pie taken up by each item

* To calculate amount from a pre-drawn pie chart, first measure the angle of the sector, then use the formula: $\dfrac{\text{angle}}{360} \times \text{total number on the pie chart}$

* To calculate the angle to draw your own pie chart, first use the formula:

  angle given to each item = 360° ÷ total number on the pie chart

  Then to calculate the angle for an individual sector:

  angle for a sector = angle given to each item × number of items in that sector

N O T E S

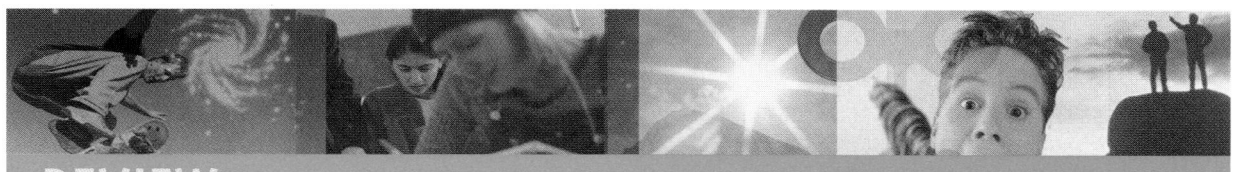

REVIEW

1. The pie chart shows the eye colour of 180 pupils.

   a. How many pupils have blue eyes?
   b. What fraction of the total number have green eyes?
   c. How many have grey eyes?
   d. What is the most common eye colour?

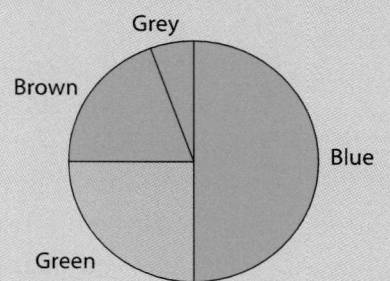

2. 100 ml of milk is made up as follows:

Protein	3.4 g
Carbohydrate	5 g
Fat	1.7 g

   Show this information on a pie chart. (Recall that g is the abbreviation for grams.)

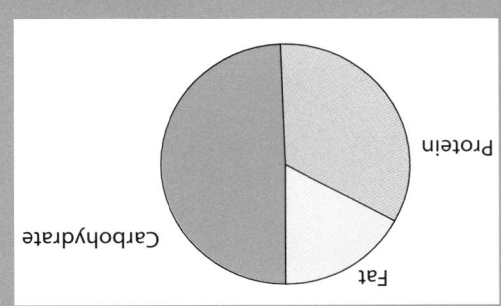

Answers

1. a. Half the pie chart represents blue eyed people, this is 180 ÷ 2 = 90 people
   b. A quarter ($\frac{1}{4}$) of the total number had green eyes
   c. 20° of the pie chart represents grey eyed people: $\frac{20}{360} \times 180 = 10$ people
   d. the most common eye colour is blue.

2. Total amount represented on the pie chart = 3.4 + 5 + 1.7 + = 10.1 grams.

   So angle per gram = 360° ÷ 10.1 = 35.6°.

   (Note that this is a rounded number. You should store the unrounded number in the memory of your calculator and use this when calculating the angles for each sector. See N22, Degrees of Accuracy.)

   So the sector angles are as follows. (Round each one to the nearest whole number of degrees.)

Protein	3.4 × 35.6° = 121°
Carbohydrate	5 × 35.6° = 178°
Fat	1.7 × 35.6° = 61°

   Check that they add up to 360°: 121 + 178 + 61 = 360.

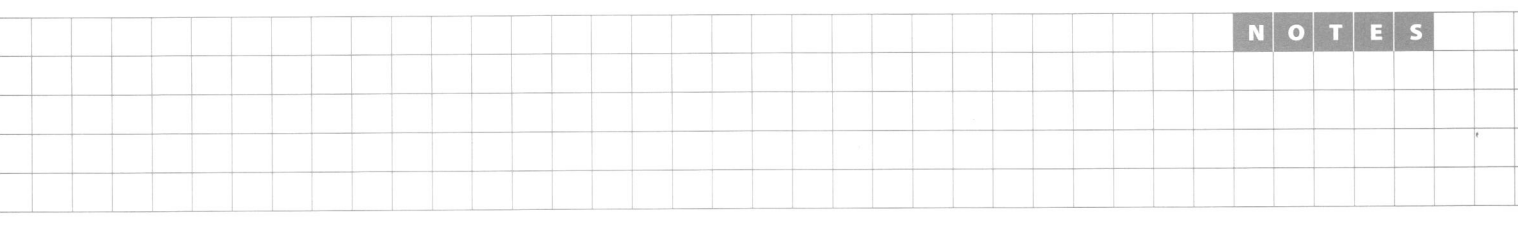

H6	Conversion Graphs	H6

There is often a need to convert a measurement given in one unit into a measurement given in a second unit. For example, when you go on holiday to Spain it is useful to be able to convert the cost of something you are buying from pesetas into pounds to see if it is a good bargain.

Sometimes temperature is given in degrees Celsius and sometimes in degrees Fahrenheit, so it is useful to be able to convert one to the other.

Distances on mainland Europe are given in kilometres and in the UK they are given in miles.

Conversion can be done numerically. It can also be done using a conversion graph.

EXAMPLE

Draw a conversion graph that changes miles to kilometres (km), given that 5 miles is 8km.

If 5 miles is 8km, we can calculate some more values very easily.

10 miles is 2 × 8km = 16km
20 miles is 4 × 8km = 32km, and so on
0 miles is 0km

This gives us a number of points to plot on a graph, so let's plot these points. When choosing the scale, remember that we want to be able to use our conversion graph to convert quite large distances. This means we need to go up at least 100 miles.

We plot miles going horizontally up to 100, and kilometres vertically up to 160 (see ● A4, Coordinates). Plot (0, 0), (5, 8), (10, 16) and (20, 32).

We find that these points all lie on a straight line. It is essential that the line is very accurately drawn. This is difficult if all the points are clustered together in the bottom left-hand corner of the graph. To make it accurate, it is a good idea to plot one point quite far up the graph. If we know that 10 miles is 16km, then 100 miles is 160km.

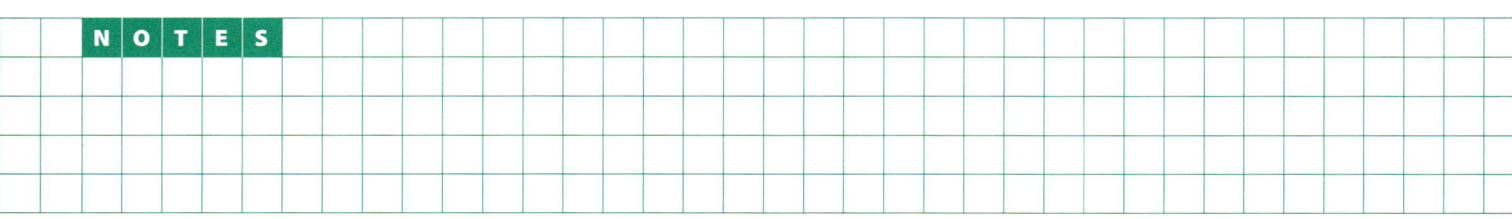

I have plotted the point (100, 160) to enable me to draw the line accurately.

We can now use the graph to convert miles into kilometres, and kilometres into miles.

To convert 25 miles into kilometres, draw a straight line up from the 25 miles point on the miles axis until it hits the line of the graph. Then draw a horizontal line from the graph to the kilometres axis and read off the value. This is the number of kilometres in 25 miles. We read off that 25 miles is 40km.

To convert 148km into miles, go across from 148km until you hit the graph and then down to the miles axis. Read off that 148km is about 92 miles.

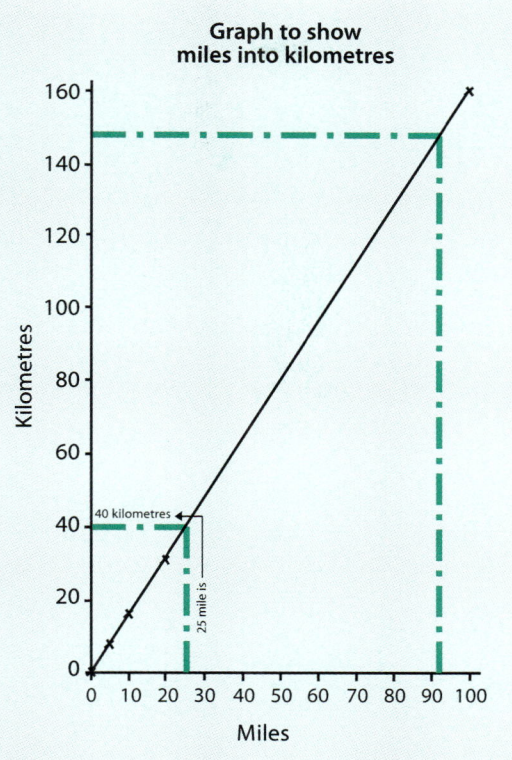

Graph to show miles into kilometres

Even if you are very accurate, it is important to know that conversion graphs only give you an estimate of the conversion. To be exact, you need to use numerical methods.

KEY CONCEPTS

Use conversion graphs to convert one unit into another ✳

To draw a conversion graph, plot two or more points from the information given, and then join them up with a straight line ✳

Remember, conversion graphs do not always go through (0, 0). Do not assume that they do ✳

To use a conversion graph, find the amount you are converting on one scale. Then draw a line straight up or along from this point until you hit the graph. Read off the other unit from the other scale at this point ✳

N O T E S

REVIEW

1. Draw a conversion graph to convert degrees Celsius (°C) into degrees Fahrenheit (°F). Use the facts that 0°C is 32°F, and 100°C is 212°F.

My grandmother used to talk about the year when the temperature went up to 100°F. She said it was the hottest year ever. The weather forecast now always gives the temperature in °C and I want to know how hot 100°F is in °C so I can see if we break my grandmother's record. Use your graph to find out.

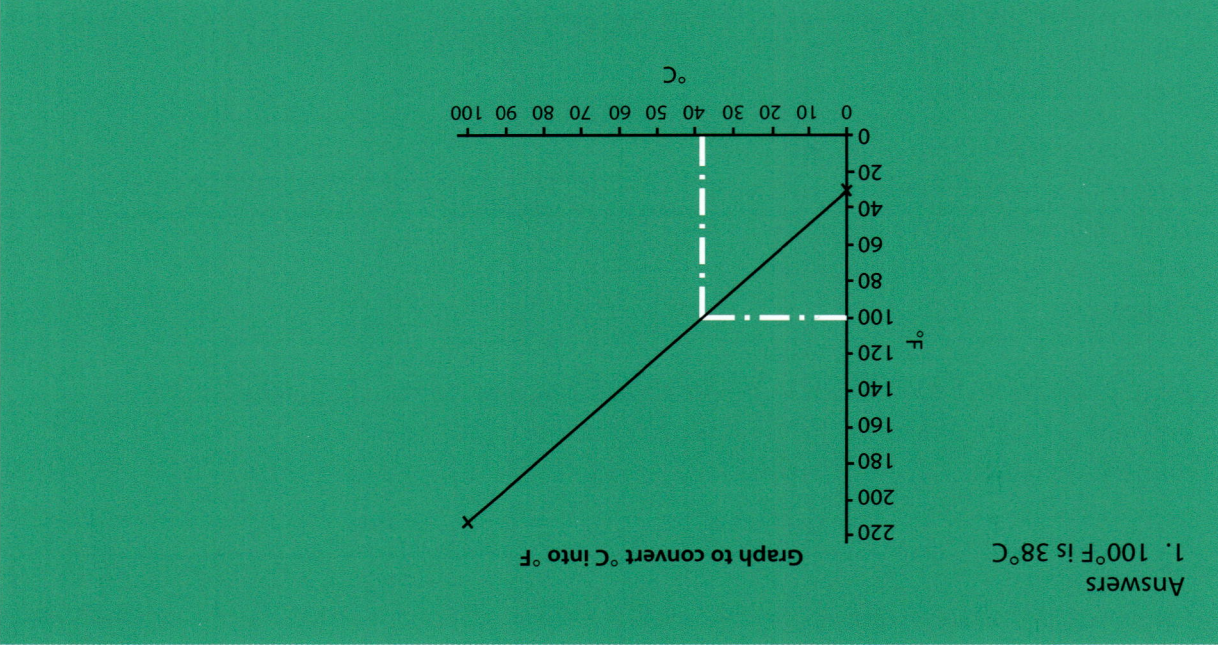

Graph to convert °C into °F

Answers

1. 100°F is 38°C

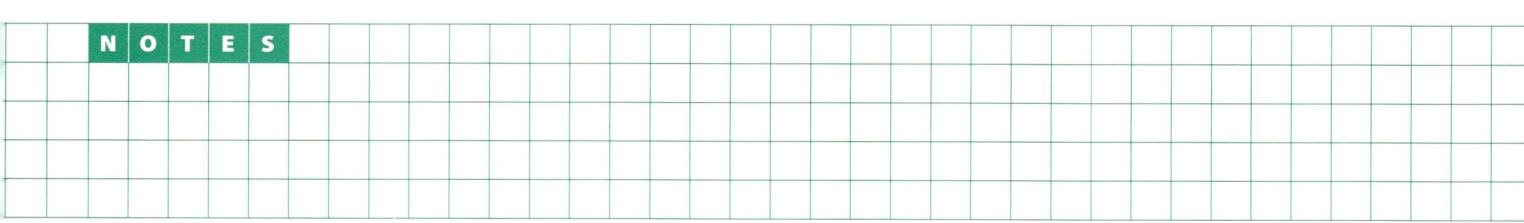

H7 Scatter Graphs H7

Scatter graphs are drawn to show the relationship between two types of data. They can be used to help you prove or disprove various hypotheses, such as:

- The taller you are, the longer toes you have
- Big animals weigh more
- The more TV you watch, the cleverer you are
- The more goals scored by a football team, the more points gained in the league table

Let's investigate one of these theories.

EXAMPLE 1: BIG ANIMALS WEIGH MORE

The weights and sizes of various animals are listed below:

Animal	Size (cm)	Weight (kg)
Aardvark	120	55
Baboon	70	23
Badger	75	12
Cheetah	120	55
Kangaroo	165	90
Koala	85	12
Leopard	150	90
Orang-utan	100	75
Sloth	60	40
Giant tortoise	100	150
Wombat	105	30

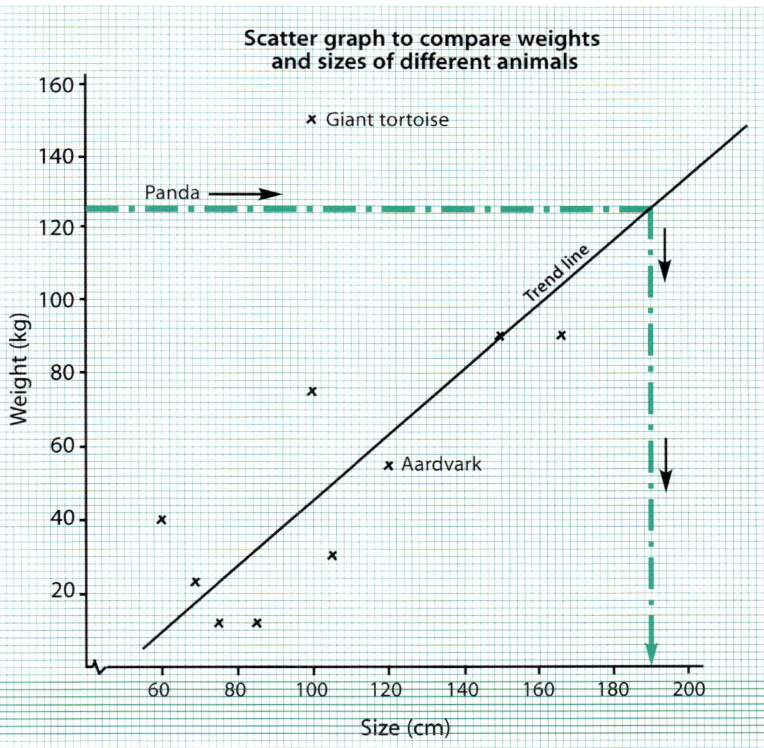

Scatter graph to compare weights and sizes of different animals

The scatter graph opposite compares weight and size. Each data value is plotted as a point.

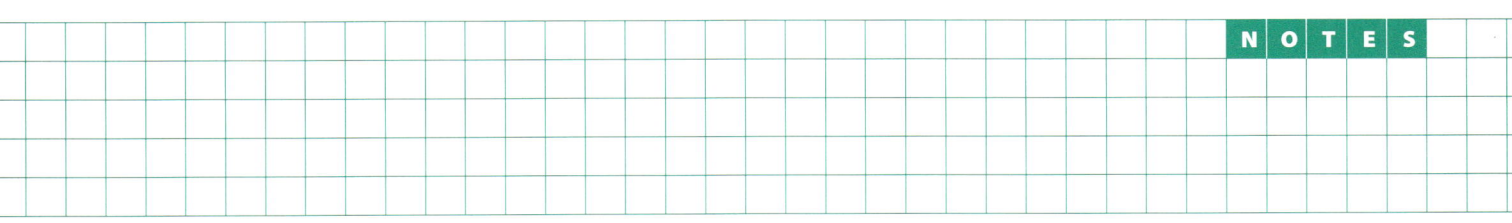

The aardvark weighs 55 kg and measures 120 cm. So the point representing the aardvak is plotted at coordinate point (55, 120). (This is 55 across and 120 up; see ◖ A4, Coordinates.)

The graph shows that there is a relationship between weight and size. The points go roughly in a line in a positive direction. This means that the bigger the animal is, the more it weighs. Our hypothesis is true.

We say that there is a **positive correlation** between weight and size.

Not all the data fit into the pattern. Can you see the animal that does not fit well into the data? Can you say why?

The point that is out of line with the rest is at (100, 150). This is the giant tortoise. It is probably out of step because size has been defined as height. A tortoise is not very tall, but is certainly very heavy for its height!

A panda weighs 125 kg. We can use our scatter graph to predict how big we expect it to be. Draw in a trend line through the points. This line should go through as many points as possible and there should be roughly the same number of points above the line as below the line. Ignore any points that do not fit the pattern (the giant tortoise).

This line is called a **line of best fit**.

To predict how big a panda is, draw a line across from a weight of 125 kg until you hit the line of best fit. Draw a vertical line downwards to the size axis. Read off the value. A panda must be about 190 cm tall.

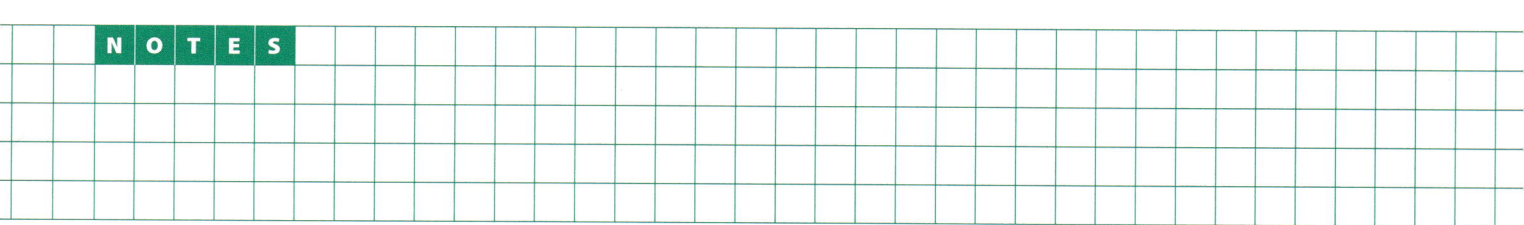

N O T E S

EXAMPLE 2: THE MORE TV YOU WATCH THE CLEVERER YOU ARE

This is a difficult hypothesis to test, because it is difficult to measure *cleverness*. Nishma decided to measure cleverness by counting how many GCSE passes each person had. She collected data from ten people, showing the number of hours of television they watch in a week and the number of GCSE passes they achieved.

Number of hours of TV per week	5	25	15	10	20	15	35	20	30	10
Number of GCSE passes	10	5	8	8	6	6	2	4	6	5

The scatter graph below shows the relationship between hours of television watched and number of GCSE passes.

It is a different relationship from that in Example 1.

The more television the people watched, the fewer GCSE passes they obtained. We say there is a **negative correlation** between amount of TV watched and the number of GCSE passes obtained.

But can we conclude that our hypothesis is true? The graph seems to **disprove** it.
It actually seems to show that the **less** TV you watch, the cleverer you are.

We have to be very careful making this type of conclusion. It is probably true that the more TV you watch, the less time you have to study for exams. This would mean that you pass fewer exams. But we cannot conclude that *watching TV* makes you less clever!

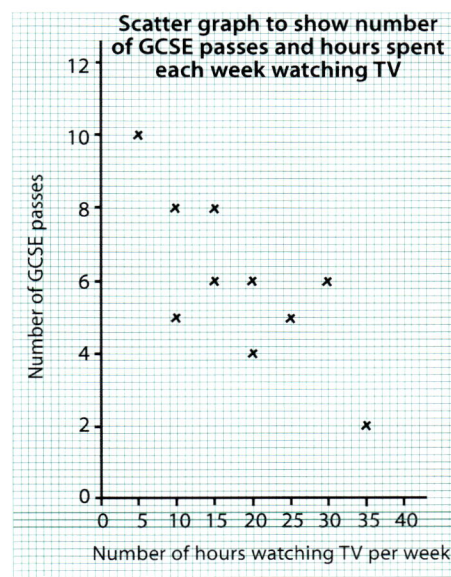

Scatter graph to show number of GCSE passes and hours spent each week watching TV

THINK ABOUT IT

Look back at the graph for time watching TV and GCSE passes. Would the pattern of data (the *trend line*) continue forever?
How many GCSE passes would you expect, according to the graph, from a person who watched TV for 50 or more hours per week?
Also, how much TV would you expect a person to watch who passed 12 or more GCSEs?
Are these predictions *realistic*?

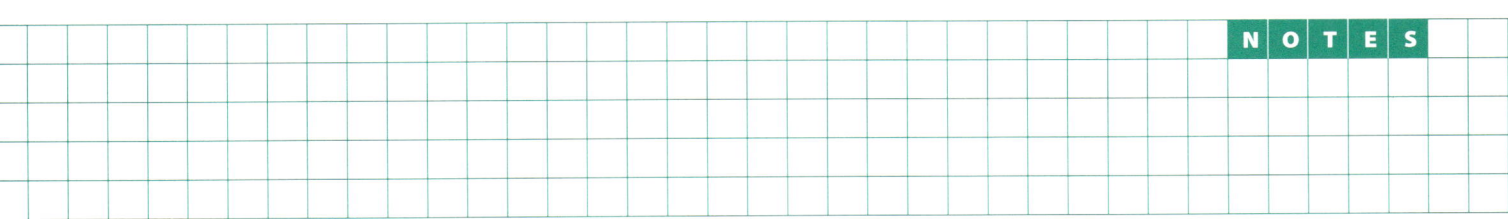

✳ Types of relationship

There are three main types of relationship:

- **Positive correlation**
  This means that as one variable gets bigger, the other gets bigger too.

  A perfect positive correlation is where all the points lie on a straight line.

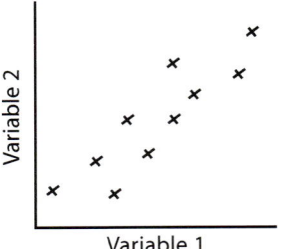

- **Negative correlation**
  This means that as one variable gets bigger, the other gets smaller.

  A perfect negative correlation is where all the points lie on a straight line.

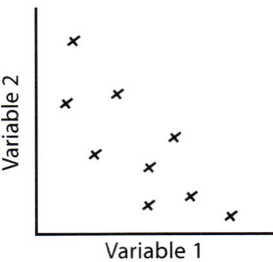

- **No correlation**
  The points are scattered randomly.

  There is no relationship between the two variables.

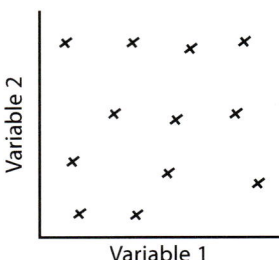

KEY CONCEPTS

✳ Scatter graphs are plotted to show relationships between two sets of variables

✳ Each pair of variables is plotted as a coordinate point

✳ There are three main types of scatter graph, showing:
positive correlation
negative correlation
no correlation

✳ A line of best fit, also known as a trend line, can be drawn through the points to help you make predictions about other data where only one variable is known

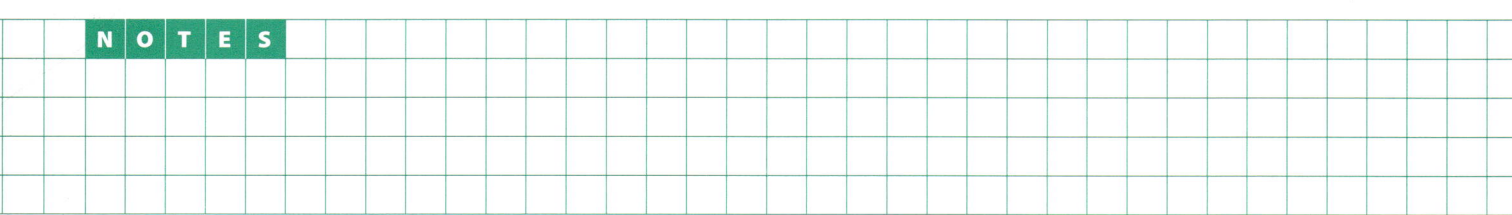

N O T E S

REVIEW

1. One morning, Sara found a huge footprint in her garden. It was 50cm long. She couldn't imagine what sort of creature had made it. She decided to try to predict how big the creature must be. She gathered together all her friends and measured their feet and their heights. She obtained the following data:

Size of feet (cm)	24	30	15	29	22	27	18	20	28	25
Height (m)	1.60	1.80	1.40	1.72	1.65	1.70	1.54	1.50	1.75	1.67

Plot a scatter graph of foot size against height for Sara's data. Draw foot size going horizontally from 15cm up to 50cm. Draw height going vertically from 1.40m to 2.30m.
Use your graph to predict how tall Sara's mysterious night time visitor was.

2. What type of relationship would you predict for the following pairs of variables?
Do a sketch of what you think the graph would look like.

   a. Height and toe size
   b. House number and ability in mathematics
   c. Number of goals scored by a football team and total points score
   d. Number of hours spent on the computer and time taken to complete all levels of a computer game
   e. The air temperature and the number of hot drinks sold

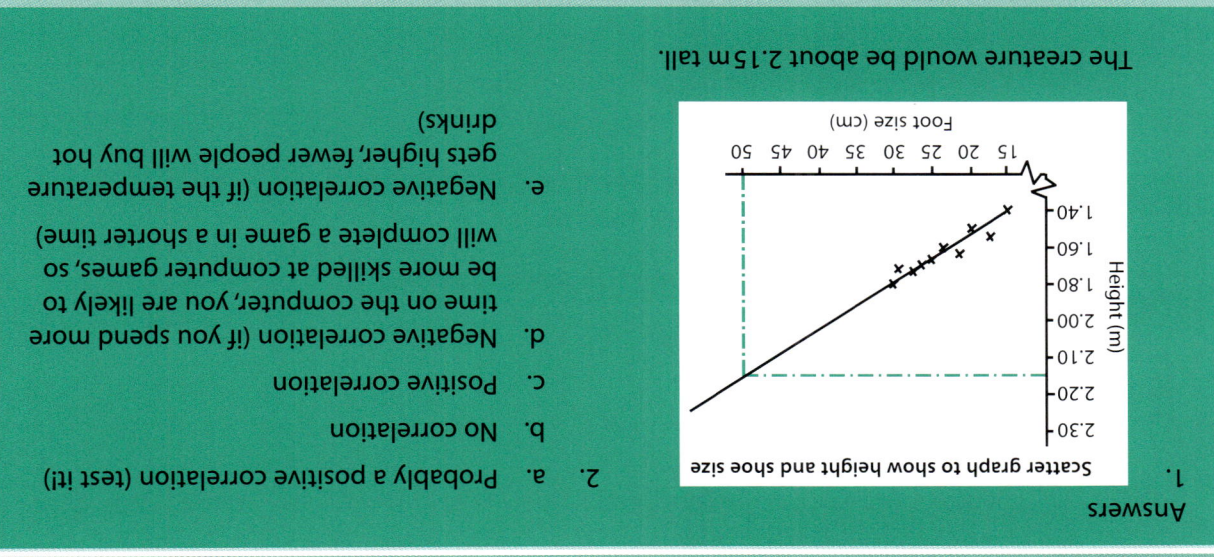
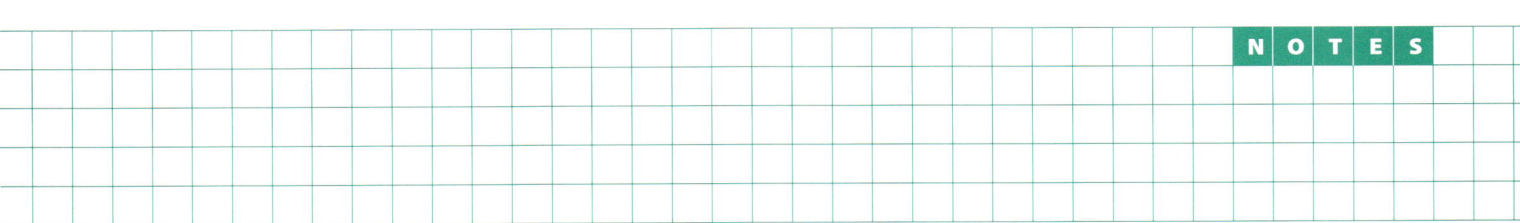

H8	Averages	H8

What springs to mind when you think of the word 'average'?
You may think 'usual', 'most common' or 'typical' perhaps.

DID YOU KNOW?

The average length of a dog's tail is 10cm.

The average number of children per family is 2.4 (what a strange thought!)

On average, most people like strawberry ice-cream.

Keep these ideas in mind when reading this section.

How can we find the 'average'? There are two simple types of average that can be used: the mode and the mean.

 ## The mode

We may decide to use the most frequently occuring value. This only works if there is an obvious value that comes up most often. This is called the mode.

The table gives the numbers of pairs of shoes of different sizes bought in a shop.

More people bought a size 6 shoe than any other size (ten people), so 6 is the mode shoe size.

On a pie chart, the mode would be represented by the biggest sector. On a bar chart it would be the longest bar.

Size	Frequency
3	2
4	5
5	6
6	10
7	4

DID YOU KNOW?

Think of the word 'modern': can you see why it sounds like 'mode'? A modern set of clothes is what most people are wearing. Also *la mode* is French for fashion.

N O T E S

✳ The mean

What if there isn't an obvious 'most common' or 'mode' average?

A group of six friends get together to go to the cinema. The tickets cost £5 each, but the friends all have different amounts of money. They each turned out their pockets and counted the money they had on them. They had: £5, £3, £7, £6, £1 and £8.

Could they afford to go if they shared out the money equally? If they did that, they would each get the mean average amount. The richest person would have to give some money to the poorest person. First imagine them all throwing the money in together.

The total amount is then £5 + £3 + £7 + £6 + £1 + £8 = £30

If they share out the money equally they will each get £30 ÷ 6 = £5.

So they can all go!

This average is called the **mean**. Think about the mean being when you share out everything evenly (so you **aren't** being mean!). In this example we found the total amount of money and then divided it by the number of people.

Mean average = total amount of all the data added up
÷ total number of items

DID YOU KNOW?
Can you imagine the process of sharing out the number of children per family? This is why we sometimes end up with rather odd results. Sharing out a total of ten children between four families gives $2\frac{1}{2}$ children each! Ouch!

✳ The range

When looking at averages it is also important to look at how spread out the data are, as the next example will show. This is called the **range** of the data.

Imagine a game of cricket. If you want to know who are the best batsmen you may need to think about how consistent they are. It is no good having a cricketer who may be able to score centuries but very rarely does so; especially if the rest of the time he scores nothing! You would be taking a chance putting him on your team!

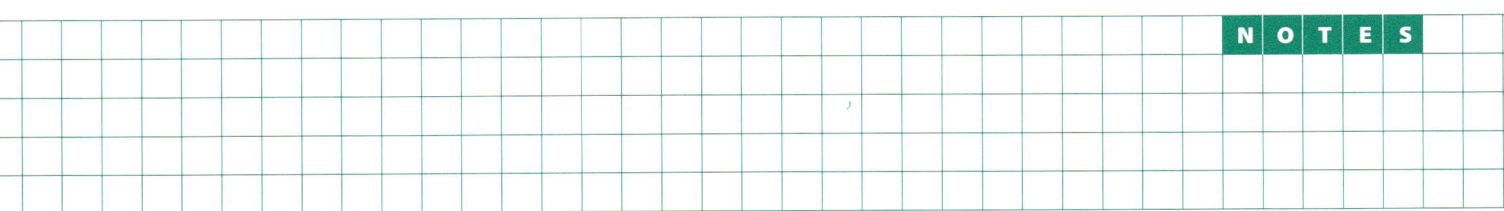

N O T E S

EXAMPLE   Vikram is a fantastic batsman. Only last week he scored a century!
His scores for the latest season are:

101	0	0	1	3	0	0	2	112	1

Fred does the job quite well, but I've never seen him scoring a century.
His scores were:

23	23	20	23	22	23	21	23	22	21

Calculate Vikram and Fred's batting average.

Remember you have to share out all their runs equally between each of their games.
They each played ten games in total.

Vikram's total number of runs is 101 + 0 + 0 + 1 + 3 + 0 + 0 +2 + 112 + 1 = 220 runs.
His average is 220 over ten games so that's 220 ÷ 10 = 22 runs per game.

Fred's total number of runs is 23 + 23 + 20 + 23 + 22 + 23 + 21 + 23 + 22 + 21 = 221
runs. His average is 221 ÷ 10 = 22.1 runs per game.

THINK ABOUT IT

Fred's average score makes sense, because looking at his scores you see his average is
'typical' of his scores. But what about Vikram's? Is his average 'typical' of his scores
as a whole?

So who is the better batsman? Their average scores are about the same. Who would
you rather have in your team? I would rather have Fred, as Vikram is a bit of a gamble
as he may score nothing!

We have found the mean number of runs for each player to determine batting average,
but in this case the range is also a measure of how consistent a player is.

Range = highest number – lowest number

This gives us the 'gap' between the highest and the lowest numbers

Vikram's range is 112 – 0 = 112
Fred's range is 23 – 20 = 3

There is a huge difference in the ranges. Fred is *far* more consistent because he has the
smaller range.

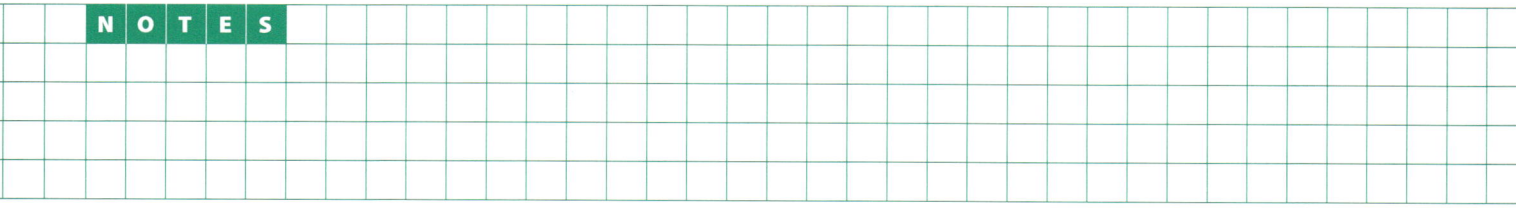

N O T E S

DID YOU KNOW?

It is important for manufacturers to make ranges as small as possible. For example, imagine if a roll of toilet paper had an average mean of 500 sheets per roll but a range of 100 sheets. Then the smallest roll you could buy could have up to 100 sheets fewer than the largest!

Wouldn't you be lucky to get the roll with 550 sheets? On the other hand, imagine if you had bought the one with only 450 sheets! I think the toilet roll manufacturer would get a lot of complaints!

KEY CONCEPTS

The average is the number that is 'typical' of the data. The average can be expressed as the mode or the mean depending on the set of data you have. (We will deal with a third average, called the median, later) ✳

The mode is the most common value ✳

You work out the mean by sharing all the values out equally, or:
mean = total of all the values added together ÷ the number of values you have ✳

The range is a measure of how spread out a set of data is. It can be used to say how consistent a set of measurements or scores are. You work it out as: range = highest value – lowest value ✳

REVIEW

1. The pie chart gives the number of people who bought different dog foods. Which is the mode dog food?

2. The number of goals scored by two footballers over five matches are as follows

   Michael Owen   0, 3, 1, 0, 2
   Alan Shearer   0, 0, 1, 0, 2

   Work out the mean score and their range.

N O T E S

3. Two companies make boxes of matches. They both claim to have, on average, forty matches per box. Take ten boxes at random. The number of matches per box is:

    Smatch   39, 40, 40, 41, 40, 39, 41, 40, 41, 39

    Strike it!   35, 42, 43, 36, 41, 35, 45, 40, 44, 35

    SMATCH
    AVE CONTENTS:40

    Work out the average number of matches for each company to see if you agree with their claim. You will need to find the mean, the mode and the range. Which company has the largest range? Which company would you buy matches from?

HIGHER PERFORMANCE

1. 'The average number of arms a man has is two.' Is this talking about *mode* average or *mean* average?

2. Three people have a mean average age of 60 years. Two of them are aged 55 and 62. How old is the third person?

3. Three friends share out some money equally. They get £15 each. The range of the three amounts is £4. What could the three original amounts have been?

Answers

1. Bark has the biggest section, so it is the mode.

2. Michael's mean is 6 ÷ 5 = 1.2 goals per game. His range is 3.
    Alan's mean is 3 ÷ 5 = 0.6 goals per game.
    His range is 2.

3. Smatch's mean is 400 ÷ 10 = 40, so their claim is true. Their range is 41 − 39 = 2 so they are pretty consistent. Their mode is also 40, since more boxes have 40 in than any other amount.
    Strike it's mean is 396 ÷ 10 = 39.6 which is very nearly 40, so their claim looks just about true. Their mode is only 35, however! I would be doubtful of their claim. Their range is 45 − 34 = 11. They are not very consistent. I would definitely buy from Smatch.

Answers

1. Mode average, as most people have two arms but not everyone. A mean average would probably be 1.9999999…

2. 63 years old. A mean age of 60 years would mean that if their ages were shared out equally they would all be 60 years old. Their total age would therefore be 60 + 60 + 60 = 180 years. One person was 55 and another is 62, so that's 117 years used up, leaving 180 − 117 = 63 years old for the third person.

3. They could be £13, £15 and £17. To check this, note that the mean is £15 (obvious since the person with £17 could give £2 to the person with £13 leaving them all with £15). The range is £17 − £13 = £4 as required.

H9 — Averages from Grouped Data — H9

In ◐ H8, Averages, we learnt how to calculate the mean average from a set of data.

In real-life situations you get a far better picture of the average if you have a lot of data. Companies who do market research use hundreds and hundreds of pieces of data.

How can we find the mean average of this much data? We would have to add up lots and lots of numbers, which would take a very long time. There must be an easier way.

Look back at ◐ H1, Collecting Data. We looked at an example about the winnings paid out by a game at a fair. The amounts paid out in pence for the first fifteen people were:

$$10, 5, 0, 5, 5, 0, 0, 0, 10, 5, 0, 0, 0, 0, 50$$

To find out the average we could look at the results and say that a pay-out of 0p was the most common. Thus 0p is the mode average pay-out.

Let's also calculate the mean.

Adding up all the amounts, $10 + 5 + 0 + 5 + 5 + 0 + 0 + 0 + 10 + 5 + 0 + 0 + 0 + 0 + 50 = 90$.

Dividing by the number of pay-outs (15): $90 ÷ 15 = 6$

Thus the mean average pay-out is 6p.

THINK ABOUT IT

Which average do you think is the best one to use? Think about which one is most 'typical' of the data as a whole.

Could we have calculated the mean in another way? There must be a quicker way to total up the amounts. Look at the data again.

eight people received no pay-out:	$8 × 0p$	$= 0p$
four people received 5p:	$4 × 5p$	$= 20p$
two people received 10p:	$2 × 10p$	$= 20p$
one person received 50p:	$1 × 50p$	$= 50p$

This is $0p + 20p + 20p + 50p = 90p$ in total, as we had before.

This gives us the total in a quicker way.

Now, mean $= 90p ÷ 15 = 6p$, as before.

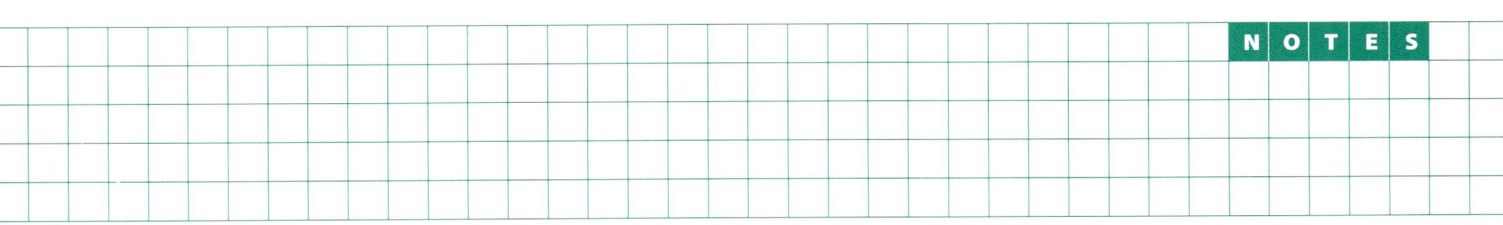

NOTES

Increasing the amount of data

Opposite is a frequency chart of the winnings of the first hundred people who played the game. Now it is in a frequency chart, we can clearly see how many of each amount was paid out.

Winnings	Frequency	Total pay-out
0p	56	0p × 56 = 0p
5p	24	5p × 24 = 120p
10p	14	10p × 14 = 140p
50p	6	50p × 6 = 300p
		Total = 560p

For example, twenty-four people won 5p, which is a total pay-out of 5p × 24 = 120p.
To find the mean average we need to share this out among all the people who played.
This means we divide by 100, as one hundred people played.
Mean average = 560 ÷ 100 = 5.6p.
The mode average is, again, 0p, since this is the most common pay-out.

EXAMPLE The following table gives the numbers of chocolate bars eaten in a week by the workers at Scoff It chocolate manufacturers. What is the mean average?

We first need to calculate how many chocolate bars were eaten in total. We then need to divide by the number of people. For example, five people ate two bars each. This gives a total of ten bars for these people. Add a third column to calculate all the totals in this way.

There's only one problem! What shall we take 'more than 7' chocolate bars to be? Two people ate 'more than 7' bars. How many bars is this, in total? Let's say *more than 7* is about 10. Thus, these two people ate about twenty bars between them.

Number of chocolate bars eaten	Frequency	Total number of chocolate bars
0	2	0 × 2 = 2
1	4	1 × 4 = 4
2	5	2 × 5 = 10
3	1	3 × 1 = 3
4	2	4 × 2 = 8
5	2	5 × 2 = 10
6	1	6 × 1 = 6
7	1	7 × 1 = 7
more than 7	2	10 × 2 = 20
Total	**People = 20**	**Chocolate bars = 2 + 4 + 10 + 3 + 8 + 10 + 6 + 7 + 20 = 70**

The mean average is calculated by dividing the total chocolate bars eaten by the number of people (like sharing the total number of chocolate bars among everyone equally).
There are twenty people altogether. This is found by adding up all the frequencies.
The mean is 70 ÷ 20 = 3.5.
On average, the workers eat three and a half chocolate bars per week.

N O T E S

✳ Grouped data

The method can also be applied to data that have been put into groups.

In ▶ H1, Collecting Data, we looked at the times of people in a local egg and spoon race. Here are the times of a race, at the Olympic egg and spoon racing games. They have been tallied off into a grouped data table.

Times (seconds)	Frequency
10–14	10
15–19	5
20–24	4
25–29	1

We know that to find the average we need to add up all the times of all the competitors and then divide by the number of competitors.

Look at the first group. Ten people ran the race in times between 10 and 14 seconds. Roughly how fast did **each** of them run the race? We don't know exactly, because the individual times aren't known. It seems fair to take the middle value as a good estimate. The middle value (or **mid-interval** value to give it its proper name) is half way between 10 and 14. This is 12. Thus, we are saying that, on average, this group ran the race in about 12 seconds.

The total time for this group is therefore 12 seconds × 10 = 120 seconds.

Let's rewrite the table so we can keep track of the totals. Introduce a column for mid-interval time and a column for total times:

Times (seconds)	Mid-interval	Frequency	Total times
10–14	12	10	12 × 10 = 120
15–19	17	5	17 × 5 = 85
20–24	22	4	22 × 4 = 88
25–29	27	1	27 × 1 = 27
	Total	**People = 20**	**Times = 320**

$$\text{Mean average} = \text{total time} \div \text{total number of people}$$
$$= 320 \div 20 = 16 \text{ seconds}$$

The mode time can't be quoted for sure, but we can talk about the most common group of times. We call this the **modal group**. Here, the modal group is 10–14 seconds.

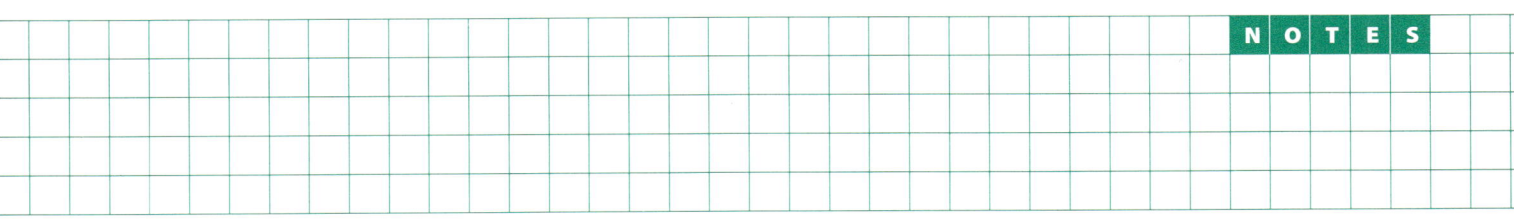

THINK ABOUT IT

Look back at the table for the local egg and spoon race in ● H1, Collecting Data. What is the mean average for these people?

What can you say about the egg-carrying skills of the two groups of people?

KEY CONCEPTS

✳ You may have to find the mean from a table of data. This is usually when there is too much data to write it in a long list

✳ When finding the mean from a table, remember the formula for calculating the mean:
mean = total of all the pieces of data ÷ number of data values

✳ In a table: total of all the pieces of data = the total of all the (data values × frequency of that value)
number of data values = total frequency

✳ When finding the mean of grouped data, approximate the data value by finding the midpoint of the group first. Then: total of all the pieces of data = the total of all the mid-interval values × frequency of that value

✳ The modal group is the group with the greatest frequency in a grouped data chart

REVIEW

1. Some pupils were conducting a survey on the environment. They collected data on the number of people travelling in cars. Here are their data:

Number of people in the car	Frequency
1	8
2	7
3	4
4	4
5	1
6	1

Calculate the mode and mean number of people in the car. Which average seems the most appropriate and why?

2. Calculate the mean of the following data, collected by a little known space explorer who was investigating how tall the inhabitants of the planet Zorg are in comparison with humans. Also give the modal group.

Height (m)	Frequency
$1.5 \le h < 2$	4
$2 \le h < 2.5$	10
$2.5 \le h < 3$	6
$3 \le h < 3.5$	2

NOTES

3. In section H1 we saw how Bill was interested in redesigning the library and wanted to see how high he could make the library shelves. He collected the following data on average reach height.

Calculate the mean average reach height.

How high would you recommend he build the shelves in the library?

Reach height (m)	Frequency
$1.80 \leq h < 1.90$	2
$1.90 \leq h < 2.00$	3
$2.00 \leq h < 2.10$	4
$2.10 \leq h < 2.20$	6
$2.20 \leq h < 2.30$	4
$2.30 \leq h < 2.40$	4
$2.40 \leq h < 2.50$	1
$2.50 \leq h < 2.60$	1

Answers

1.

Number of people in the car	Frequency	Total number of people
1	8	$1 \times 8 = 8$
2	7	$2 \times 7 = 14$
3	4	$3 \times 4 = 12$
4	4	$4 \times 4 = 16$
5	1	$5 \times 1 = 5$
6	1	$6 \times 1 = 6$
Totals	Cars = 25	People = 61

Mean average = $61 \div 25 = 2.44$ people per car.

Mode average is the most common number of people per car, which is one person per car.

The mean average is a better average to use because it best represents the data.

2.

Height (m)	Mid-interval	Frequency	Mid-interval × frequency
$1.5 \leq h < 2$	1.75	4	$4 \times 1.75 = 7$
$2 \leq h < 2.5$	2.25	10	22.5
$2.5 \leq h < 3$	2.75	6	16.5
$3 \leq h < 3.5$	3.25	2	6.5
Total		22	52.5

Mean average = $52.5 \div 22 = 2.39$ m (rounded to the nearest centimetre).

The modal group is $2 \leq h < 2.5$.

This means heights are greater than or equal to 2m and less than 2.5m.

3.

Reach height	Mid-interval	Frequency	Mid-interval × frequency
$1.80 \leq h < 1.90$	1.85	2	$1.85 \times 2 = 3.7$
$1.90 \leq h < 2.00$	1.95	3	5.85
$2.00 \leq h < 2.10$	2.05	4	8.2
$2.10 \leq h < 2.20$	2.15	6	12.9
$2.20 \leq h < 2.30$	2.25	4	9
$2.30 \leq h < 2.40$	2.35	4	9.4
$2.40 \leq h < 2.50$	2.45	1	2.45
$2.50 \leq h < 2.60$	2.55	1	2.55
Total		25	54.05

Mean average = $54.05 \div 25 = 2.16$m.

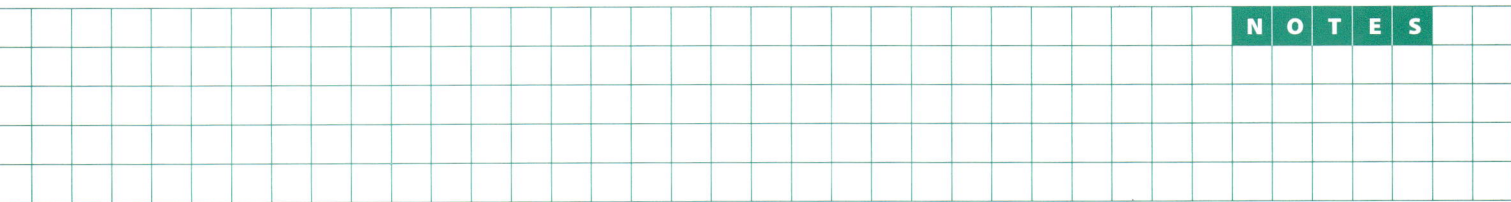

N O T E S

H10   Cumulative Frequency   H10

In this section we meet a third type of average: the median. The **median** is the middle data value. Its use is best illustrated by an example.

The weekly wages of nine people who work in Shopper's Paradise are:

    120   121   119   115   122   450   123   118   116

The mean average wage is calculated to be £156 (you check this!). This is not very representative of the data, since no one in the shop earns this amount. The reason why the mean works out to be so unrepresentative is because there is one person who earns a lot (probably the manager of the shop). When you calculate the mean, this large value distorts the final value. It is not a good average to calculate because of this distortion.

There is no mode since they all earn different amounts.

We need a third type of average. If you look at the data, it looks as if the average wage should be about £120. This is roughly the middle value.

If the wages are all put into order, from smallest to biggest, we can pick out the middle value more exactly:

    115   116   118   119   **120**   121   122   123   450

The middle wage is £120. This is called the median wage. It is far more representative of the data.

The median is the middle value when all the data values are put in order.

If there are an odd number of values it is easy to pick out the middle value. If there are an even number of values, the median is the value half way between the two middle values.

EXAMPLE   The wages of ten people working at The Jolly Eater, a restaurant, are:

    110   130   400   50   120   80   100   125   90   115

Find the median wage.

Put the wages in order from smallest to biggest:

    50   80   90   100   110   115   120   125   130   400

The median lies half way between the two middle values. These are £110 and £115. The value half way between is calculated by the formula: $\dfrac{110 + 115}{2} = 112.50$

The median wage is £112.50.

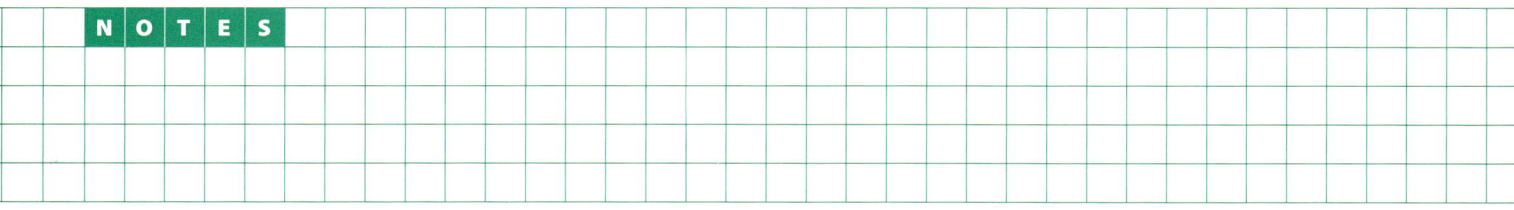

✳ Larger sets of data

The data below were taken from Greengrocer's International, a company who checks the lengths of cucumbers in different countries. The lengths of cucumbers in England were measured to see if they were acceptable. The measurements of thirty cucumbers selected at random are:

Length of cucumber (cm)	Frequency
26	1
27	2
28	7
29	9
30	6
31	3
32	2

THINK ABOUT IT

At this stage we are able to calculate such statistics as mean and mode from data presented in this way (see section ▶ H9, Averages from Grouped Data). Try it! You should get the mean to be 29.1 cm and the mode is 29 cm.

We can find the median of these data by looking at the table and calculating where the 'half-way value' lies. There are thirty pieces of data. The half-way value, the median, is half way between the fifteenth and sixteenth values when the cucumbers are put in order of length. The list would start like this:

26, 27, 27, 28, 28, 28, 28, 28, 28, 28, 29, 29, 29, 29, 29, 29, 29, 29, 29, 30, 30, … and so on …

It would be a very long list! We have actually gone as far as we need to go, as we have found the fifteenth cucumber. It is 29 cm long. The sixteenth is also 29 cm long. The median is therefore 29 cm.

Another way to get the median is to calculate the **cumulative frequency**. Look back at the data.

One cucumber was 26 cm long or less.
Three cucumbers were 27 cm long or less. (One was 26 cm and two were 27 cm long.)
Ten cucumbers were 28 cm long or less. (One was 26 cm, two were 27 cm long and seven were 28 cm long.)

Continuing this pattern we can start to see roughly where the fifteenth cucumber will lie.

Let's put the results into a table.

Length of cucumber (cm)	Frequency	Cumulative frequency	
26	1	1	= 1
27	2	3	= 1 + 2
28	7	10	= 1 + 2 + 7
29	9	19	= 1 + 2 + 7 + 9
30	6	25	= 1 + 2 + 7 + 9 + 6
31	3	28	= 1 + 2 + 7 + 9 + 6 + 3
32	2	30	= 1 + 2 + 7 + 9 + 6 + 3 + 2

Ten cucumbers were 28 cm long or less.
Nineteen cucumbers were 29 cm long or less.
The fifteenth value and sixteenth value must have landed in the 29 cm group.
This shows that the median is 29 cm, as we calculated before.

 ## Calculating the median from grouped data

The table opposite illustrates times taken for a variety of chewing gum to lose its taste. Eighty sticks of chewing gum were chewed and the times recorded.

A cumulative frequency table will show how many pieces of chewing gum last less than a certain time. Five sticks lasted for less than 10 minutes. Seventeen (5 + 12 = 17) sticks lasted for less than 20 minutes, and so on. The cumulative frequency table looks like this:

Time (min)	Frequency
$0 \le t < 10$	5
$10 \le t < 20$	12
$20 \le t < 30$	45
$30 \le t < 40$	15
$40 \le t < 50$	3

Times (less than)	Cumulative frequency	
10	5	= 5
20	17	= 5 + 12
30	62	= 5 + 12 + 45
40	77	= 5 + 12 + 45 + 15
50	80	= 5 + 12 + 45 + 15 + 3

The median is the time that the middle stick lasted for. This occurs in the $\frac{80}{2}$th position; the 40th position.
Seventeen sticks lasted for less than 20 minutes.
Sixty-two sticks lasted for less than 30 minutes.

The time taken by the fortieth stick lies somewhere between 20 and 30 minutes. The median time therefore lies somewhere between these two times. We cannot read it exactly from a table. We use a **cumulative frequency graph** to estimate it more exactly.

N	O	T	E	S

Drawing a cumulative frequency graph

We plot the times against the cumulative frequency on a graph. The cumulative frequency values are always plotted vertically.

Plot the times on the horizontal axis. Look closely at how I have done this. I have plotted the time axis as a continuous scale in steps of 10 minutes. I have then plotted how many sticks lasted for **less than** that time, at each multiple of 10 minutes. A smooth 'lazy S' line should now be drawn through all of the data points. This line is known as an **ogive**.

The ogive can now be used to estimate lots of statistics about the data, as well as the median. Remember, the curve tells you how many sticks lasted for **less than** a certain time.

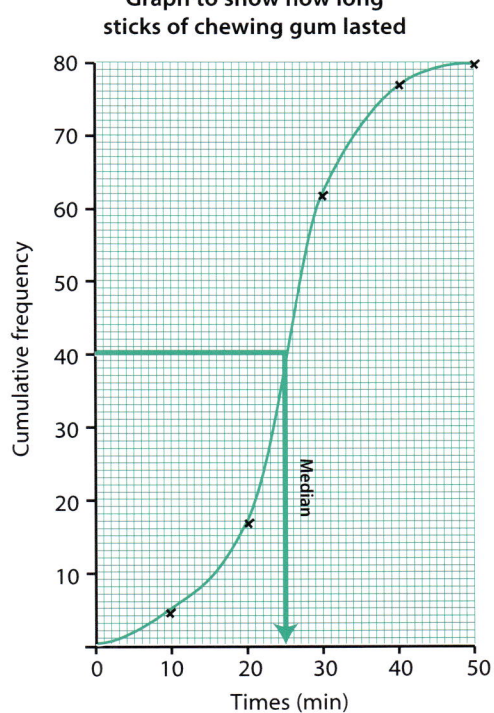

Graph to show how long sticks of chewing gum lasted

Median

The median is the middle value. We need to look at the half-way point of the data. We estimated this, from our table, as between 20 and 30 minutes. Our graph will give us a much more accurate value.

The median occurs at the half-way position. This is called the fiftieth **percentile** because it lies 50% of the way through the data.

> 50% of 80 = 40, so the fiftieth percentile of a cumulative frequency of 80 is at the fortieth position.

If we draw a line on the graph across from a cumulative frequency of 40 and down to the Times axis we can read off a good estimate of the median. The median time is 25 minutes. On average, the chewing gum lasts for 25 minutes.

Remember that this is a 'less than' graph. This means that we can also say that 50% of the chewing gums last for 25 minutes or less.

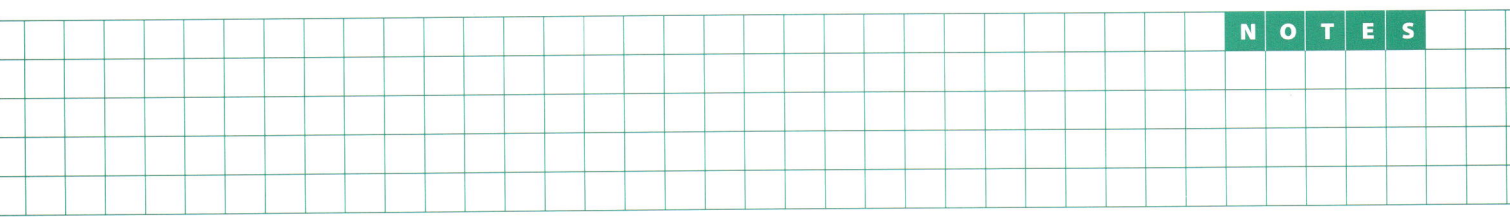

N O T E S

51

 # Measure of Spread

There is another important measurement we can estimate from the ogive. This is a measure of the spread or the dispersion of the data. It is called the inter-quartile range.

Looking at the data we can see that most sticks of chewing gum last for 20 to 30 minutes. The measurements seem to be bunched up around the middle. There are fewer values at the extremes.

The inter-quartile range looks at how spread out the middle 50% of the data is. Companies use the inter-quartile range as a measure of consistency of a product. The smaller the spread happens to be, the more consistent the product. This means that more of the items are around the average and there are fewer extreme values.

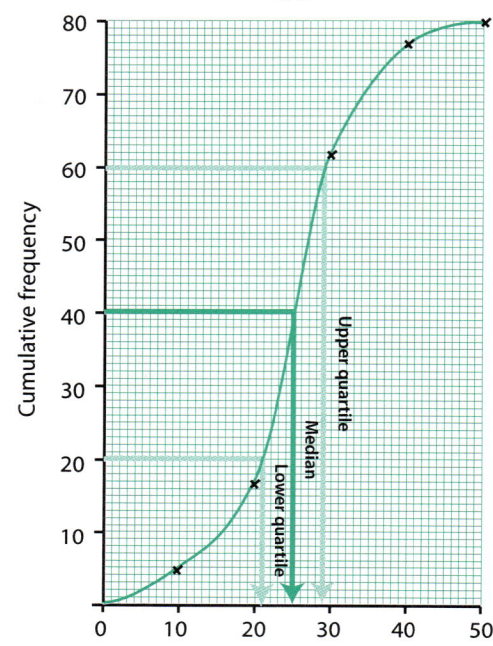

Graph to show how long sticks of chewing gum lasted

Inter-quartile range

The lower quartile is calculated in the same way as the median, except it gives the value one quarter of the way up the data. This is known as the twenty-fifth percentile.

25% of 80 = 20, so the twenty-fifth percentile of a cumulative frequency of 80 is at the twentieth position.

Go across at 20 and read off the Times axis.
25% of the chewing gum sticks last for 21 minutes or less.
The lower quartile is 21 minutes.

The upper quartile is calculated in the same way as the median, except that it gives the value three-quarters of the way up the data. This is known as the seventy-fifth percentile.

75% of 80 = 60, so the seventy-fifth percentile of a cumulative frequency of 80 is at the sixtieth position.

Go across at 60 and read off the Times axis.
75% of the chewing gum sticks last for 29 minutes or less. The upper quartile is 29 minutes.
So the lower quartile is 21 min and the upper quartile is 29 min. The middle 50% of the sticks last between 21 and 29 minutes. The inter-quartile range tells how far apart these two values are.
To calculate the inter-quartile range, use the formula:

inter-quartile range = upper quartile – lower quartile

Here, inter-quartile range = 29 – 21 = 8 minutes. If this was a larger value, it would show that the times that the chewing gum lasts for vary more. The flavour would be more inconsistent. There would be more variance in the times of the middle 50% of the data.

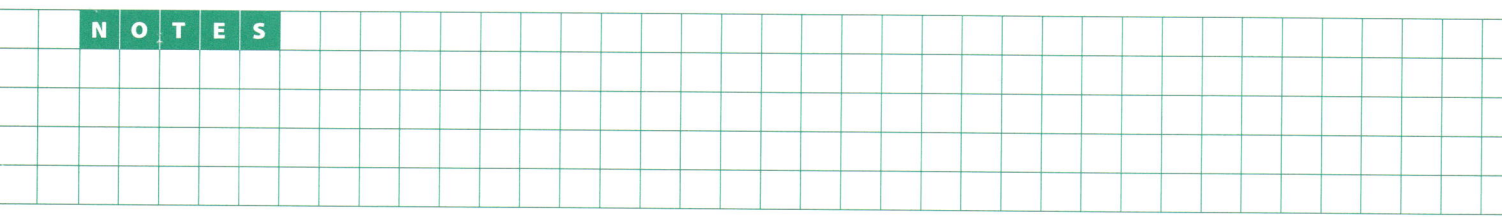

N O T E S

 Other questions

You can read much more from the graph than just the average and the interquartile range.

Question 1

Regulations say that a chewing gum company should not sell chewing gum that lasts less than 12 minutes. How many sticks of chewing gum lasted for 12 minutes or less? What percentage of the stock is this?

Our graph will give us an accurate estimate. If we use our ogive and draw a line up from 12 minutes until we reach the ogive we can read off the frequency of sticks that lasted for 12 minutes or less.

Reading off, we get the result that approximately seven sticks lasted for 12 minutes or less.

As a percentage, this is $\frac{7}{80} \times 100\% = 8.75\%$.

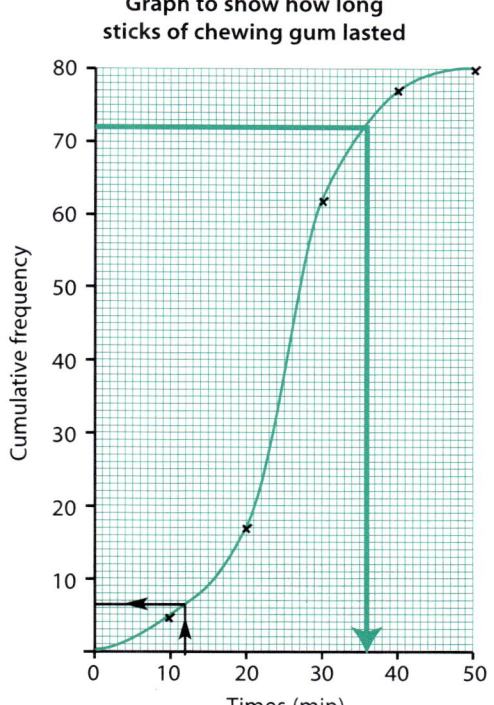

Graph to show how long sticks of chewing gum lasted

So 8.75% of the company's chewing gum is below the regulation!

Question 2

The 10% of the chewing gum that lasted for longest may qualify for a company record. How long do the top 10% last for?

The top 10% of the chewing gum is the top eight sticks (10% of 80 is 8).

We need to read off from 80 − 8 = 72 sticks.

Reading off, seventy-two sticks last for less than 36 minutes.

So the top 10% last for 36 minutes or more.

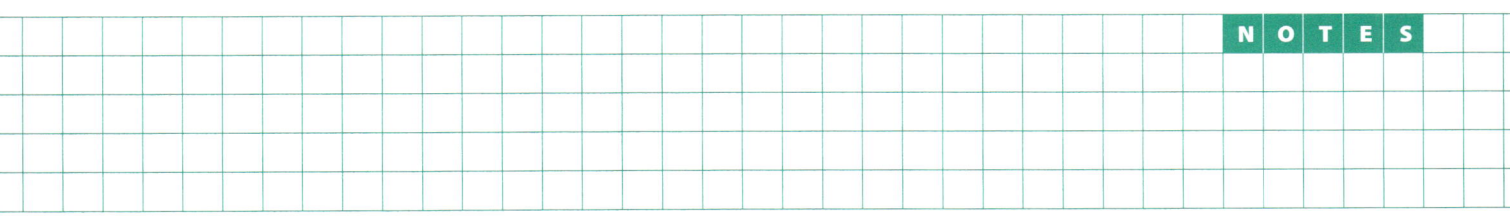

N O T E S

KEY CONCEPTS

✳ A cumulative frequency table is constructed by calculating a running total of the frequency. This is the number of data values that are less than a particular amount

✳ A graph should be drawn of the cumulative frequency with a smooth curve, called an **ogive**, connecting all points

✳ The **median** is the data value that lies at the half-way point. Calculate 50% of the total number of data values and use the graph to read the value off the x-axis. Then 50% of the data are equal to or less than this measurement

✳ The **lower quartile** is found by using the twenty-fifth percentile. Calculate 25% of the total and read off the measurement that corresponds to this value

✳ The **upper quartile** is used by finding the seventy-fifth percentile. Calculate 75% of the total, and read off the measurement that corresponds to this value

✳ The **inter-quartile** range gives an indication of how spread out the middle 50% of the data are. To calculate this use the formula: **inter-quartile range = upper quartile – lower quartile**

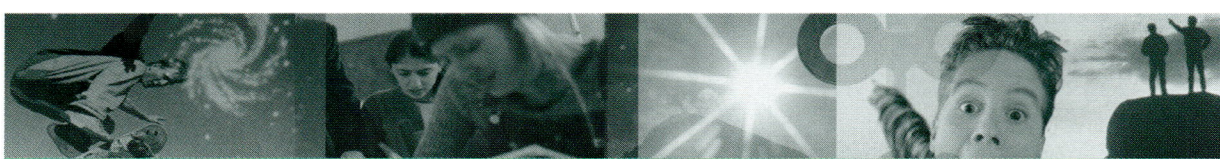

REVIEW

1. The following table shows the weights of pet dogs owned by forty people:

   a. Copy and complete the cumulative frequency table.

   b. On graph paper draw the cumulative frequency graph for the data.

   c. Use the curve to estimate:
      i   the median average weight of the dogs
      ii the upper quartile
      iii the lower quartile
      iv the inter-quartile range

   d. Comment on your results.

Weight of dog (kg)	Frequency	Cumulative frequency
0 less than 5	3	3
5 and less than 10	12	15
10 and less than 15	10	
15 and less than 20	9	
20 and less than 25	4	
25 and less than 30	2	

N O T E S

Answers

1. a.

Weight of dog (kg)	Frequency	Cumulative frequency
0 less than 5	3	3
5 and less than 10	12	15
10 and less than 15	10	25
15 and less than 20	9	34
20 and less than 25	4	38
25 and less than 30	2	40

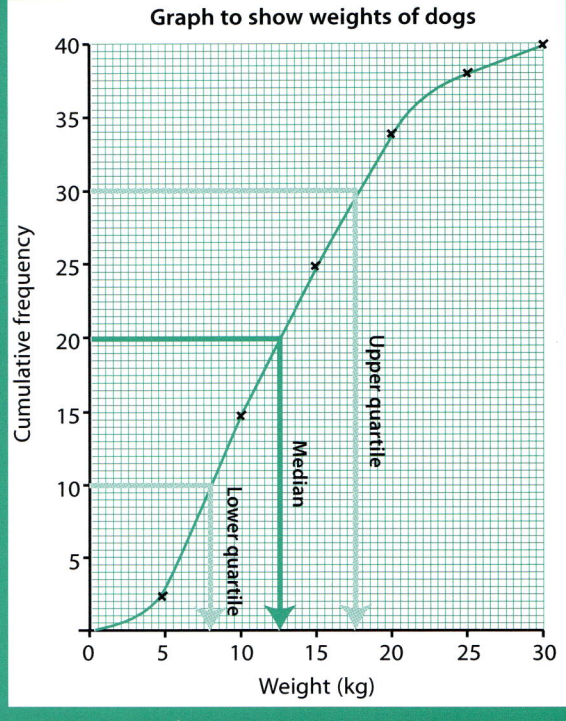

Graph to show weights of dogs

b. When plotting the graph, remember it is a **less than** graph.
Three dogs weighed less than 5 kg.
Plot weight 5 against cumulative frequency 3.
Fifteen dogs weighed less than 10 kg.
Plot weight 10 against cumulative frequency 15.

c. i The median occurs at the twentieth position. Reading off the curve, the median is 12.5 kg

ii The lower quartile occurs at the tenth position. The lower quartile is 8 kg.

iii The upper quartile occurs at the thirtieth position. The upper quartile is 17.5 kg.

iv The interquartile range is 17.5 − 8 = 9.5 kg.

d. The average weight of a dog is 12.5 kg, and 50% of the dogs have a weight between 8 kg and 17.5 kg.

HIGHER PERFORMANCE

1. These data were taken from the Racket Pro company who produce badminton racquets. The lengths of the racquets were measured correct to the nearest centimetre to see if they were acceptable.

Length of racquet (cm)	Frequency
55	1
56	3
57	13
58	21
59	15
60	5
61	2

a. Draw a cumulative frequency curve and calculate the median and the inter-quartile range.

b. For the production process to be accepted as reliable, 50% of the racquets must be no more than 1 cm different in length. Comment on how reliable the production process is.

c. The shortest allowable length for a badminton racquet is 57 cm. What percentage of the racquets were to be too small to be sold?

2. Find a set of five data values with a mode of 4, a median of 5 and a mean of 6.

Answers

1. a. Because the measurements are rounded to the nearest centimetre, a rounded length of 55 cm can be as big as 55.5 cm.

Our cumulative frequency table looks like:

Length of racquet (cm) (less than)	Cumulative frequency
54.5	0
55.5	1
56.5	4
57.5	17
58.5	38
59.5	53
60.5	58
61.5	60

b. The first point should be plotted at a length of 54.5 cm and a cumulative frequency of 0.

The second point should be plotted at a length of 55.5 cm and a cumulative frequency of 1.

The median occurs at the thirtieth position. It is 58.15 cm.

The lower quartile occurs at the fifteenth position. It is 57.4 cm.

The upper quartile occurs at the forty-fifth position. It is 58.9 cm.

The interquartile range is 58.9 cm − 57.4 = 1.5 cm.

The production process is not very reliable. The middle 50% of the racquets are 1.5 cm different in length. This is more than the 1 cm allowed.

c. In reverse, now find 57 cm on the length axis and go up until you meet the ogive. Then read the answer off the cumulative frequency axis. Reading off, we find that ten racquets were less than 57 cm. This is a percentage $\frac{10}{60} \times 100\% = 16.7\%$. Roughly 17% of racquets could not be sold.

2. The values are: 4, 4, 5, a, b where a and b can take any values that add up to 17. For example, 4, 4, 5, 6, 11 would work.

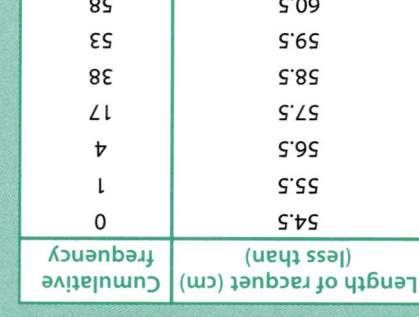

Graph to show lengths of badminton racquets

NOTES

H11   Histograms   H11

In ▶ H4, Frequency Distributions, Histograms and Frequency Polygons, we learnt how to plot a frequency diagram (histogram) for grouped data. In all our examples, the groups were all the same size. For example, ages of people lay in groups spanning 10 years. This meant that it was easy to see the number of people (the frequency) from the graph, as it was simply represented by the height of the bar. All the bars were the same width, and so a **bigger** bar was simply a **taller** bar.

In reality, surveys sometimes need to cover a large range of data, and groups of the same width are not always appropriate.

Suppose we did a survey of the number of people of different ages buying food at a supermarket. We might set up age categories as follows:

In reality, as you can see, you would find very few people in the first and last categories, and lots in the middle ones. It is better, therefore, to keep the categories in the middle section as they are, but to merge together the categories at the ends. This gives a better spread of people in the groups.

Age	Frequency
0 and up to 10	1
10 and up to 20	3
20 and up to 30	9
30 and up to 40	7
40 and up to 50	5
50 and up to 60	2
60 and up to 70	2
70 and up to 80	2
80 and up to 90	1
90 and up to 100	0

Hence a better way to group the ages is:

Age	Frequency
0 and up to 20	4
20 and up to 30	9
30 and up to 40	7
40 and up to 60	7
60 and up to 100	5

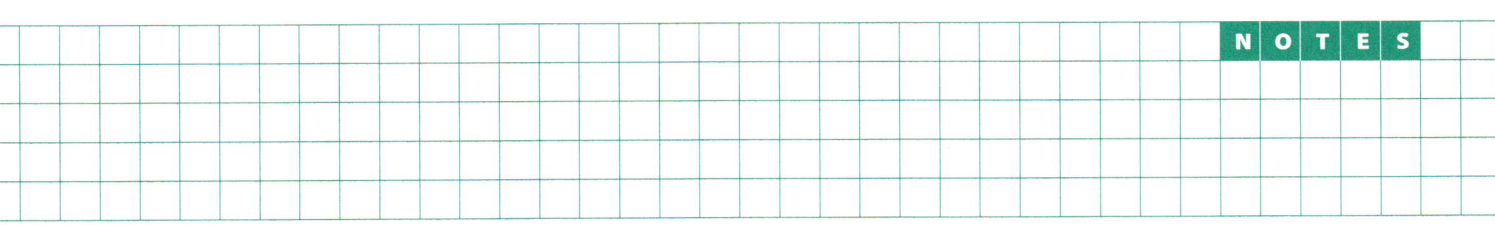

We can plot a graph of this, as we did before.

This looks very misleading! The last bar (age 60 to 100) is very wide. It looks like it takes up more space than the second bar (age 20 to 30). But the second bar represents **more** people so it **should** look bigger.

Also, look at the third and fourth bars. They both represent seven people, but one is twice as big as the other!

Up until now we have only plotted the height of the bar as the frequency. We now need to consider another factor: the **width** of the bar. These two factors combine to give the **area** of the bar. We need to take into account the **area** of the bar as well as the height.

In a histogram the **area** of the bar is the number of people (frequency).

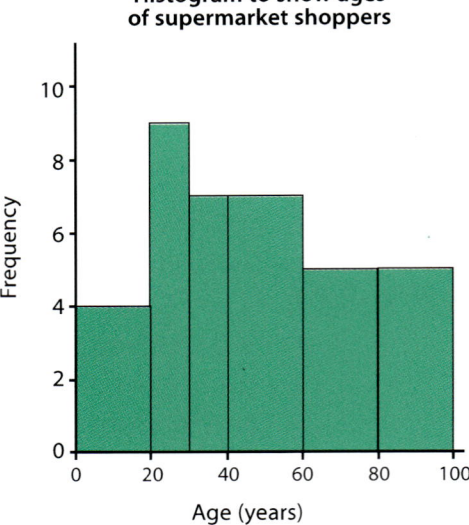

Histogram to show ages of supermarket shoppers

In this graph, the second bar should have an area of 9. The width of the bar is 10 (since the group goes from age 20 to 30; a gap of 10 years). Hence, the height of the bar should be $9 \div 10 = 0.9$.

This value is called the **frequency density**.

Check it by reversing the process. The area of the bar should be 9. Area = width × height = $10 \times 0.9 = 9$. So the bar represents nine people, as we wished.

We plot the frequency density on the vertical axis. Remember, to work this out:

frequency density = frequency ÷ width of interval

So for our example we can construct a new table:

Age	Frequency	Frequency density
0 and up to 20	4	$4 \div 20 = 0.2$
20 and up to 30	9	$9 \div 10 = 0.9$
30 and up to 40	7	$7 \div 10 = 0.7$
40 and up to 60	7	$7 \div 20 = 0.35$
60 and up to 100	5	$5 \div 40 = 0.125$

Now let's plot the histogram.

You can see now that the bars look more in proportion. The second bar looks nearly twice the size (area) of the last bar, as it is supposed to. The third and fourth bars have the same area; the fourth bar is twice as wide as the third so it is half as tall.

Do a quick check:

area of bar 1 = width × frequency density = $20 \times 0.2 = 4$

This is as we expected, as it represents four people.

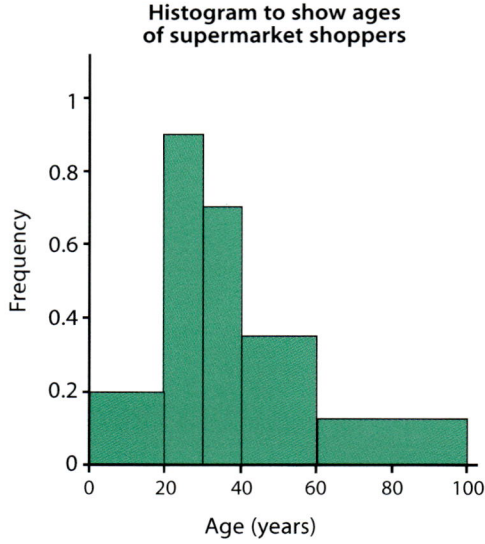

Histogram to show ages of supermarket shoppers

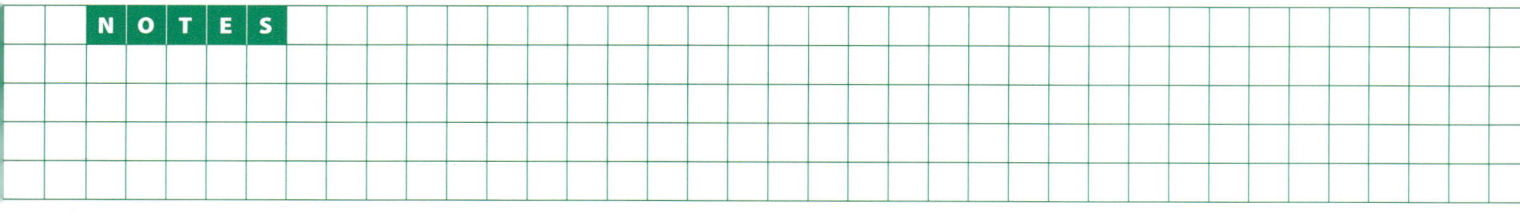

N O T E S

Reading information from histograms

You may be given a histogram and asked to find the frequency of each category.
To work out the frequency of a histogram bar, remember:

frequency is the area of bar

area of the bar = width of interval × height of bar

= width × frequency density

EXAMPLE This histogram gives the lengths of stick insects in my prize-winning collection.

How many stick insects are there in each category?

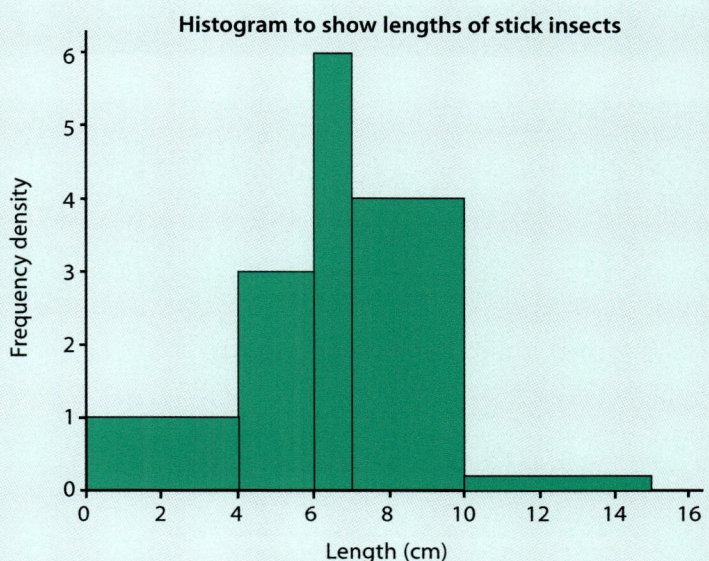

Histogram to show lengths of stick insects

Set up a table and fill it in as follows:

Length (cm)	Width of bar	Frequency density (read this off the graph)	Area of bar = frequency
0 and up to 4	4	1	4 × 1 = 4
4 and up to 6	2	3	2 × 3 = 6
6 and up to 7	1	6	1 × 6 = 6
7 and up to 10	3	4	3 × 4 = 12
10 and up to 15	5	0.2	5 × 0.2 = 1

I have four stick insects sized 0 cm and up to 4 cm.
I have six sized 4 cm and up to 6 cm.
I have six sized 6 cm and up to 7 cm.
I have twelve sized 7 cm and up to 10 cm.
I have one sized 10 cm and up to 15 cm.

KEY CONCEPTS

✳ In a histogram where the groups of data are different sizes, the area of the bar represents the frequency

✳ We plot the frequency density up the vertical axis. To work out frequency density:
frequency density = frequency ÷ width of interval

✳ To work out the frequency from a given histogram:
frequency = area of the bar
= width of interval × height of bar
= width × frequency density

REVIEW

1. Franz has just moved into a new house. When he goes into the loft he sees that it is overrun by huge spiders. Being a mathematician he decides to measure the sizes of these spiders so that he can impress his friends when they come round to visit.

He measures thirty spiders at random and the data he collects are as follows:

Leg length (mm)	Frequency
$0 \le l < 20$	4
$20 \le l < 30$	8
$30 \le l < 50$	10
$50 \le l < 70$	5
$70 \le l < 100$	3

Plot a histogram of the data that he can show to his friends.

2. The times of pupils in a primary school sack race are given in the histogram. A pupil wins a prize if his or her time is less than 40 seconds, and a booby prize if he or she takes longer than a minute. How many pupils win a prize and how many win a booby prize?

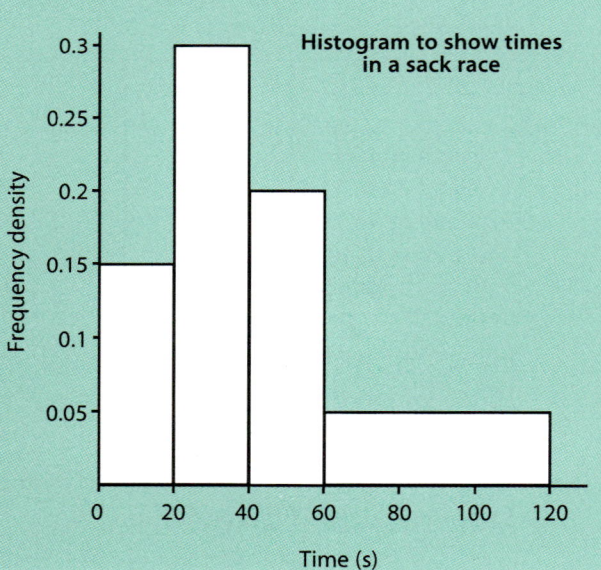

Histogram to show times in a sack race

NOTES

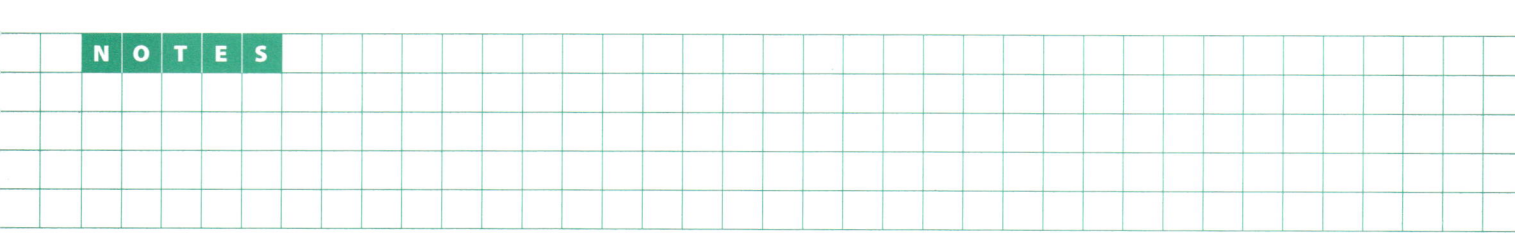

Answers

1.

Leg length (mm)	Frequency	Frequency density
$0 \leq l < 20$	4	$4 \div 20 = 0.2$
$20 \leq l < 30$	8	$8 \div 10 = 0.8$
$30 \leq l < 50$	10	$10 \div 20 = 0.5$
$50 \leq l < 70$	5	$5 \div 20 = 0.25$
$70 \leq l < 100$	3	$3 \div 30 = 0.1$

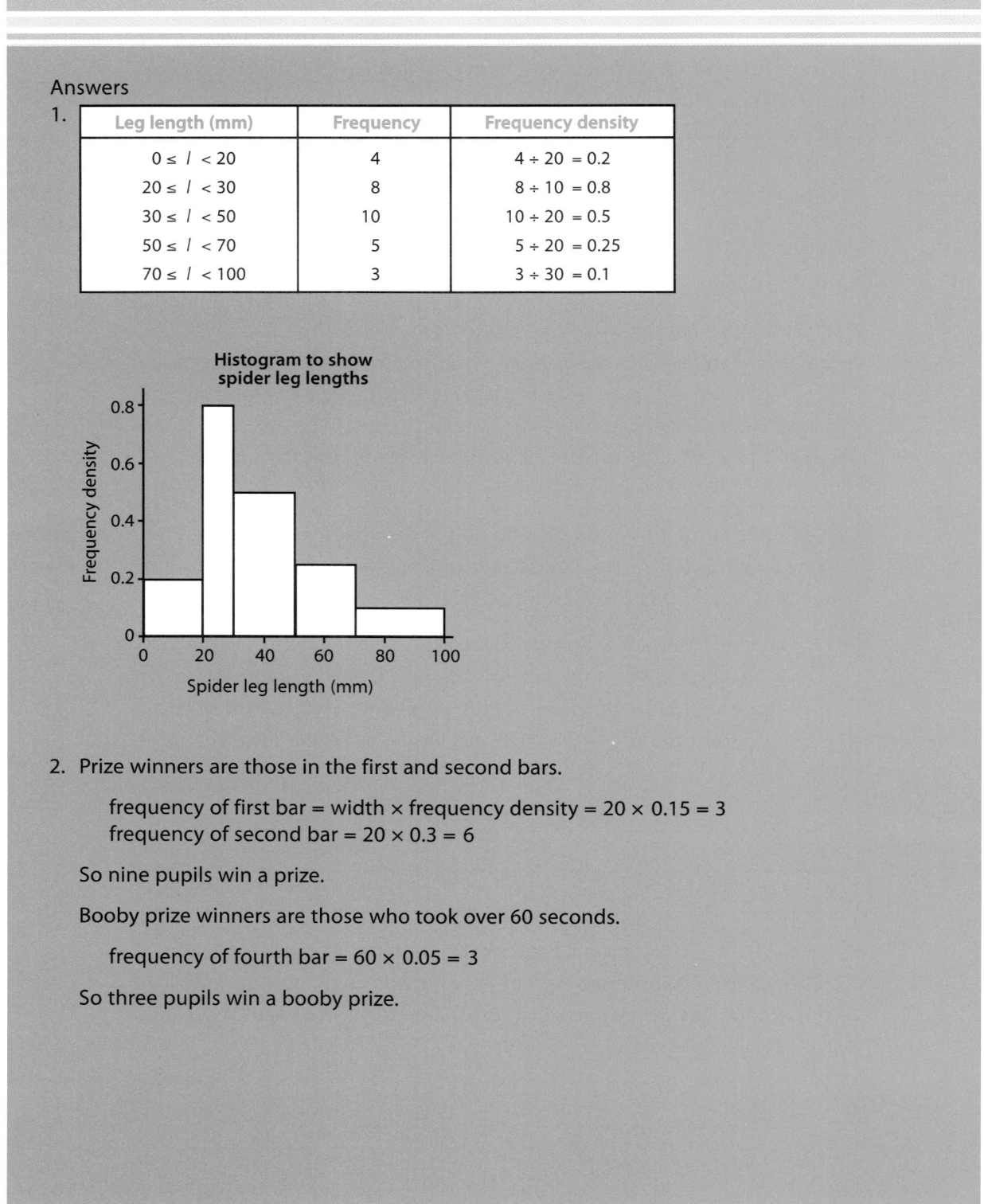

Histogram to show spider leg lengths

2. Prize winners are those in the first and second bars.

   frequency of first bar = width × frequency density = 20 × 0.15 = 3
   frequency of second bar = 20 × 0.3 = 6

   So nine pupils win a prize.

   Booby prize winners are those who took over 60 seconds.

   frequency of fourth bar = 60 × 0.05 = 3

   So three pupils win a booby prize.

H12 — Standard Deviation — H12

Below we have two sets of data from the manufacturers of badminton racquets, Shuttle Sport and Racket Pro. The badminton racquets need to be made to a specific length measured in centimetres.

Shuttle Sport	56	56	57	58	58	58	58	58	58	60
Racket Pro	56	56	59	56	56	58	58	59	59	60

Let's compare the data.

If we calculate the mean we get the value of 57.7 cm for both manufacturers. If we look at the range, the value is 4 cm for both. However, when we look at the data we get a feeling that Shuttle Sport's data are still a lot closer to the average and therefore more reliable.

One thing that we could do would be to draw two cumulative frequency graphs and measure the inter-quartile range. This will only give you a rough estimate as it will depend on how accurate you are at graph drawing.

There is another way to calculate how spread out data are, and it is called the **standard deviation**. The inter-quartile range tells us how spread out the middle 50% of the data is (see section ▶ H10, Cumulative Frequency). The standard deviation will help us to calculate accurately how spread out the middle 68% of the data is. It tells us, on average, how close the data values are to the mean average.

 ## Calculating the standard deviation

The standard deviation is calculated by averaging out the deviations from the mean. The **deviation from the mean** is the distance of a data value from the mean. The deviation of each piece of data from the mean is found by calculating:

data value − mean

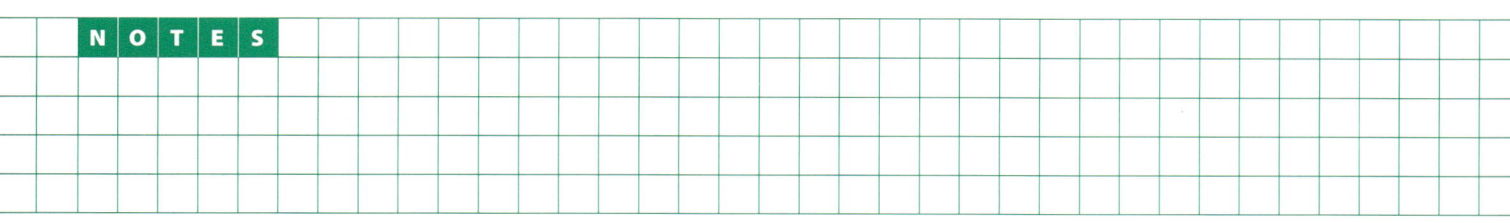

Shuttle Sport's standard deviation

The mean is calculated by normal methods; it is 57.7. The symbol for the mean is $\bar{x}$. The deviation of each data value, x, from the mean is $x - \bar{x}$.

Length of racquets (cm) x	Deviation from mean $x - \bar{x}$
56	−1.7
56	−1.7
57	−0.7
58	0.3
58	0.3
58	0.3
58	0.3
58	0.3
58	0.3
60	2.3

We want to average out all the deviations from the mean. To do this we could add up all the deviations and divide by 10. But if we do this we get:

$$\text{average deviation} = (−1.7 + −1.7 + −0.7 + 0.3 + 0.3 + 0.3 + 0.3 + 0.3 + 0.3 + 2.3) \div 10$$
$$= 0 \div 10$$
$$= 0$$

Notice that the positive and negative deviations cancel each other out!

We need to make them all positive. The way we do this is to square them before adding.

Length of racquets (cm) x	Deviation from mean $x - \bar{x}$		$(x - \bar{x})^2$
56	−1.7		2.89
56	−1.7		2.89
57	−0.7		0.49
58	0.3		0.09
58	0.3		0.09
58	0.3		0.09
58	0.3		0.09
58	0.3		0.09
58	0.3		0.09
60	2.3		5.29
		Total	12.1

Now divide by the number of racquets:

$$12.1 \div 10 = 1.21$$

We need to take the square root so we don't get an answer in square centimetres.

$$\text{standard deviation} = \sqrt{1.21} = 1.1\,\text{cm}$$

This means that (on average) the lengths of Shuttle Sport's racquets lie 1.1 cm either side of the mean, 57.7.

To be more precise, 68% of the data lies 1.1 cm to either side of 57.7 cm.
We now have two limits between which 68% of the data lies: 57.7 − 1.1 = 56.6 cm and 57.7 + 1.1 = 58.8 cm.

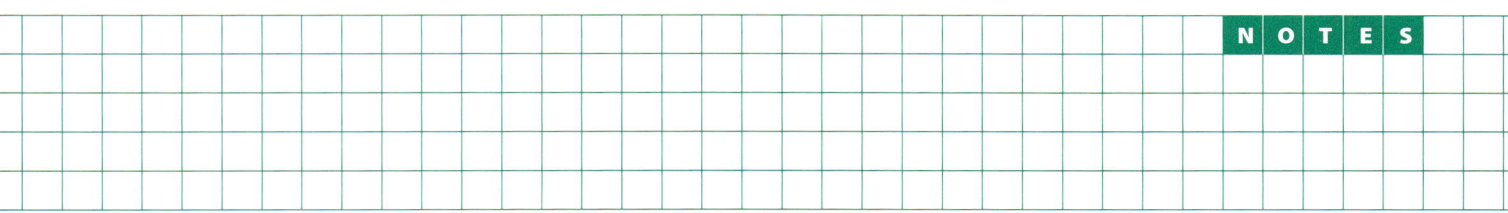

N O T E S

Let's do the same for Racket Pro. Remember, we are expecting to get a higher standard deviation, since the data look more spread out on either side of the mean.

standard deviation is

$$\sqrt{22.1 \div 10} = 1.49$$

Length of racquets (cm) x	Deviation from mean $x - \bar{x}$	$(x - \bar{x})^2$
56	−1.7	2.89
56	−1.7	2.89
56	−1.7	2.89
56	−1.7	2.89
58	0.3	0.09
58	0.3	0.09
59	1.3	1.69
59	1.3	1.69
59	1.3	1.69
60	2.3	5.29
	Total	22.1

Racket Pro's 68% lies between 57.7−1.49 = 56.21 cm and 57.7+1.49 = 59.19 cm.

These are much bigger limits and therefore back up our initial thoughts that Shuttle Sports make a product with a more consistent length.

✳ A different method

Another way to calculate standard deviation, which is simpler, is to use the equivalent formula:

$$\text{standard deviation} = \sqrt{\frac{\sum x^2}{n} - \bar{x}^2}$$

x is the symbol for the items of data
x^2 is the item of data squared
$\sum x^2$ means that you add up all the x^2 values.
n is the number of items of data
$\bar{x}$ is the mean

DID YOU KNOW?

The symbol $\sum$ is the Greek letter **sigma**. It is used in mathematics to mean 'the sum of'. Hence $\sum x^2$ means 'the sum of all the x^2 values'.

The overall formula means that you:
- Square and add all the items of data
- Divide by the number of pieces of data
- Subtract the mean squared
- Take the square root as we did before.

For example, for Shuttle Pro's racquets:

Shuttle Sport	56	56	58	58	58	58	58	58	57	60

Square and add together all the lengths first:

$56^2 + 56^2 + 58^2 + 58^2 + 58^2 + 58^2 + 58^2 + 58^2 + 57^2 + 60^2$

$= 3136 + 3136 + 3364 + 3364 + 3364 + 3364 + 3364 + 3364 + 3249 + 3600$

$= 33\,305$

$$\text{standard deviation} = \sqrt{\frac{33\,305}{10} - 57.7^2}$$

The standard deviation is 1.1 cm, as we found before.

 ## Data presented in a table

Finding the standard deviation of data in a table is more complicated, but uses the same principle of averaging the deviations from the mean.

In ▶ H9, Averages from Grouped Data, we met the pupils who were conducting a survey on the environment.

They collected data on the number of people travelling in cars. Here are their data again:

Number of people in the car	Frequency
1	8
2	7
3	4
4	4
5	1
6	1

The mean was calculated as 2.44 people per car.

The standard deviation is calculated by the formula: $\sqrt{\dfrac{\sum fx^2}{\sum f} - \bar{x}^2}$

This is an adapted version of the second formula, where $\sum x^2$ is replaced by $\sum fx^2$. (Note that fx^2 means $f \times x^2$ not $(fx)^2$.) $\sum f$ is the same as n, but has been written like this to remind you to add up all the frequencies to find the total number of data values, n.

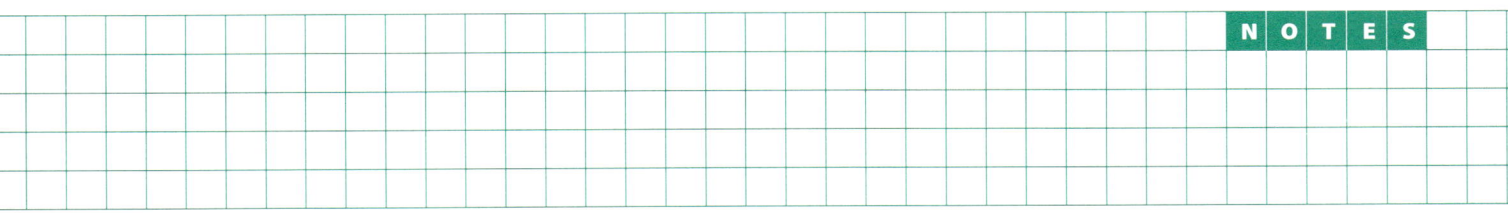

NOTES

Number of people in the car x	Frequency f	fx^2
1	8	$8 \times 1 \times 1 = 8$
2	7	$7 \times 2 \times 2 = 28$
3	4	$4 \times 3 \times 3 = 36$
4	4	$4 \times 4 \times 4 = 64$
5	1	$1 \times 5 \times 5 = 25$
6	1	$1 \times 6 \times 6 = 36$
Totals	$\sum f = 25$	$\sum fx^2 = 197$

$$\text{standard deviation} = \sqrt{\frac{\sum fx^2}{\sum f} - \bar{x}^2} = \sqrt{\frac{197}{25} - 2.44^2}$$

$$= \sqrt{7.88 - 5.9536}$$

$$= 1.39$$

This means that approximately 68% of the cars surveyed had between
$2.44 - 1.39 = 1.05$ and $2.44 + 1.39 = 3.83$ people in them.

Remember, the main use for standard deviation is to compare sets of data.
You could have surveyed cars in a different country and then compared the standard
deviations. This would give you a good comparison of how environmentally friendly each
country was.

 ## Grouped data

This works in the same way as the example above, except x is the mid-interval value of
each group.

In ▶ H9, Averages from Grouped
Data, we met the following data
showing the numbers of aliens
species of different heights. We
calculated the mean of the data as
follows:

Height (m)	Frequency x	Mid-interval f	fx
$1.5 \leq h < 2$	4	1.75	$4 \times 1.75 = 7$
$2 \leq h < 2.5$	10	2.25	$10 \times 2.25 = 22.5$
$2.5 \leq h < 3$	6	2.75	$6 \times 2.75 = 16.5$
$3 \leq h < 3.5$	2	3.25	$2 \times 3.25 = 6.5$
Total	22		52.5

$$\text{mean average} = \bar{x} = \frac{\sum fx}{\sum f} = \frac{52.5}{22} = 2.39$$

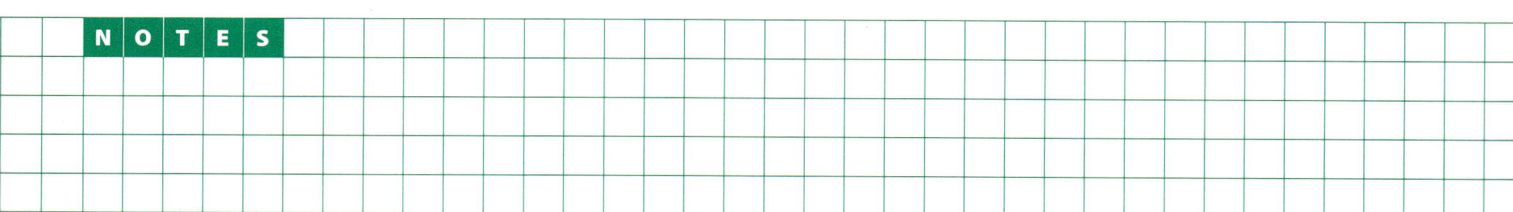

N O T E S

Add a column to the table for fx^2.

Height (m)	Frequency x	Mid-interval f	fx	fx^2
$1.5 \leq h < 2$	4	1.75	$4 \times 1.75 = 7$	$4 \times 1.75 \times 1.75 = 12.25$
$2 \leq h < 2.5$	10	2.25	$10 \times 2.25 = 22.5$	$10 \times 2.25 \times 2.25 = 50.625$
$2.5 \leq h < 3$	6	2.75	$6 \times 2.75 = 16.5$	$6 \times 2.75 \times 2.75 = 45.375$
$3 \leq h < 3.5$	2	3.25	$2 \times 3.25 = 6.5$	$2 \times 3.25 \times 3.25 = 21.125$
Total	$\sum f = 22$		$\sum fx = 52.5$	$\sum fx^2 = 129.375$

$$\text{standard deviation} = \sqrt{\frac{\sum fx^2}{\sum f} - \bar{x}^2} = \sqrt{\frac{129.375}{22} - 2.39^2}$$

$$= \sqrt{0.169}$$

$$= 0.41$$

KEY CONCEPTS

The standard deviation is a measure of how spread out a set of data is. It tells you how much the data deviate from the average ✳

To calculate the standard deviation: ✳

METHOD 1

1. Find the mean average $\bar{x} = \dfrac{\sum x}{n}$

2. Find all the deviations from the mean average $(x - \bar{x})$

3. Square the deviations $(x - \bar{x})^2$

4. Add up the squares of the deviations $\sum (x - \bar{x})^2$

5. Divide by the number of items of data

6. Take the square root

On your formulae sheet the formula for this method would look like: $s = \sqrt{\dfrac{\sum (x - \bar{x})^2}{n}}$

METHOD 2

1. Find the mean average $\bar{x} = \dfrac{\sum x}{n}$

2. Square all the items of data x^2

3. Add them up $\sum x^2$

4. Divide by the number of items of data $\dfrac{\sum x^2}{n}$

5. Subtract the mean squared.

6. Take the square root

On your formulae sheet the formula for this would look like: $s = \sqrt{\dfrac{\sum x^2}{n} - \left(\dfrac{\sum x}{n}\right)^2}$

NOTES

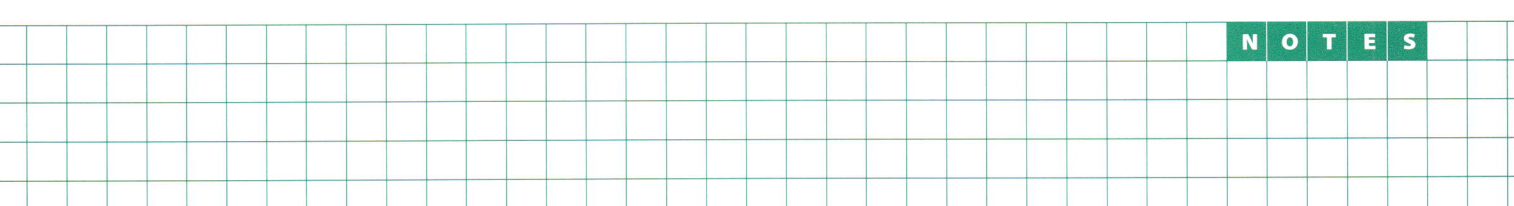

KEY CONCEPTS

✳ To find the standard deviation of grouped data

First find the mean using the formula: $\text{mean} = x = \dfrac{\sum fx}{\sum f}$

Then find the standard deviation using the formula: $s = \sqrt{\dfrac{\sum fx^2}{\sum f} - x^2}$

REVIEW

1. In H8, Averages, we had a question about two companies who made boxes of matches. They both claimed to have on average forty matches per box. I took ten boxes at random. The number of matches per box was:

    Smatch   39, 40, 40, 41, 40, 39, 41, 40, 41, 39

    Strike it!   35, 42, 43, 36, 41, 35, 45, 40, 44, 35

    Which company has the smallest standard deviation?
    Which company would you buy matches from?

2. Find the standard deviation of these data.
    They show the times of the Olympic egg and spoon race.

Time (s)	Frequency
10–14	10
15–19	5
20–24	4
25–29	1

Answers

1. **Smatch**   39, 40, 40, 41, 40, 39, 41, 40, 41, 39

$\text{mean} = 400 \div 10 = 40$

$\text{standard deviation} = \sqrt{\dfrac{39^2 + 40^2 + 40^2 + 41^2 + 40^2 + 39^2 + 41^2 + 40^2 + 41^2 + 39^2}{10} - 40^2}$

$= 0.77$

Answers cont . . .

Strike it!   35, 42, 43, 36, 41, 35, 45, 40, 44, 35

mean = 396 ÷ 10 = 39.6

standard deviation = 3.8 (by the same method)

Strike it have a lower mean average and they are also less consistent (their standard deviation is higher). I would definitely buy from Smatch.

2. Find the standard deviation of these data.
They show the times of the Olympic egg and spoon race.

Times (s)	Mid-interval time x	Frequency f	Total times fx	fx^2
10–14	12	10	$12 \times 10 = 120$	1440
15–19	17	5	$17 \times 5 = 85$	1445
20–24	22	4	$22 \times 4 = 88$	1936
25–29	27	1	$27 \times 1 = 27$	729
Total		$\Sigma f = 20$	$\Sigma fx = 320$	$\Sigma fx^2 = 5550$

mean = 320 ÷ 20 = 16 seconds

$$\text{standard deviation} = \sqrt{\frac{\Sigma fx^2}{\Sigma f} - \bar{x}^2}$$

$$= \sqrt{\frac{5550}{20} - 16^2}$$

$$= \sqrt{277.5 - 256}$$

$$= 4.64 \text{ seconds}$$

H13 | **Simple Probability** | **H13**

Before reading this section you need to make sure you understand fractions and decimals and how they relate to each other (● N11, Equivalence between Fractions, Percentages and Decimals). You also need to be able to order decimals from smallest to largest.

Measuring probability

How likely are the following events?

- If I toss a coin I will get a head
- If I spin the square spinner opposite, I will get green
- I will get an odd number on a dice
- In a bag of ten counters, where three are white and seven are green, I draw a white counter.
- The next car down the road will be red
- England will win the next World Cup

Which is the most likely? How can we compare them?

When you measure other things in mathematics it is easy to compare them, for example, who is the tallest? Just measure everyone with a ruler and compare the heights! It is not *quite* as easy for probability, but we use the same principle.

The probability line

Imagine ordering the events listed above on a line. This gives a good scale to compare probabilities, like a ruler.

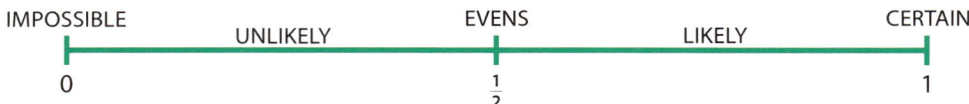

IMPOSSIBLE   UNLIKELY   EVENS   LIKELY   CERTAIN

0      $\frac{1}{2}$ 1

If an event is impossible we say it has a probability of 0; this is one end of the line.
If an event is certain we say it has a probability of 1; this is the other end of the line.

In the middle is Evens or 'fifty-fifty'. This has a probability of $\frac{1}{2}$ as a fraction, as it is half way along the line. (In decimal fractions we would say it was a probability of 0.5.) If an event has a probability of $\frac{1}{2}$, you expect it to happen half of the time.

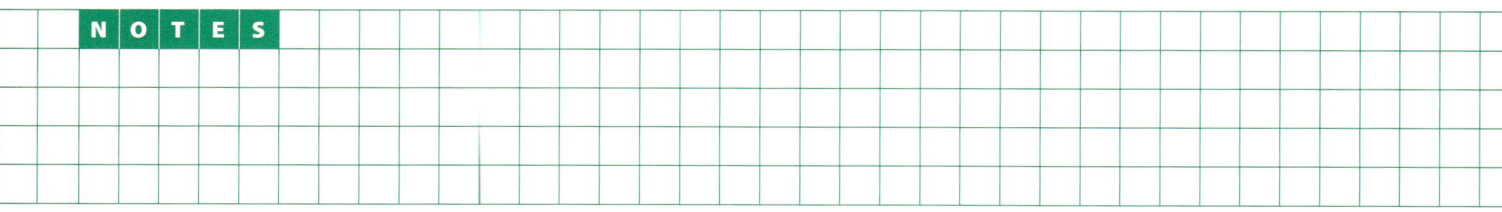

N O T E S

You can see that probabilities must always lie between 0 and 1. If you get a value larger than 1 you have done something wrong!

Writing probabilities as decimals allows us to place them accurately on a probability line. This helps us to see which events are more likely than others more easily than if we used fractions. If you are unsure of decimal fractions revise ○N10, Introduction to Decimal Fractions, and ○N11, Equivalence between Fractions, Percentages and Decimals.

Copy out the line and try to place the events listed above on it where you think they should go. Keep your answers to compare with mine.

Calculating probabilities

The coin

There are two things that could happen (events); head or tail. Each of these is equally likely. The probability of getting a head is one in two or $\frac{1}{2}$. You would expect to toss a head half of the time. This is 0.5 as a decimal. The event should be placed half way along the line, on Evens.

The spinner

The spinner will land on any of the four sections. Three out of four of them are shaded green. The fraction that is green is therefore $\frac{3}{4}$, so the probability of getting green is $\frac{3}{4}$. This goes three-quarters of the way along the line; at the 0.75 mark.

The dice

There are six possible outcomes: 1, 2, 3, 4, 5 and 6. Three of these numbers are odd (1, 3 and 5). Three out of six is half of the possible outcomes, so this also goes half way along the line, at 0.5.

Let's put these three events on the line:

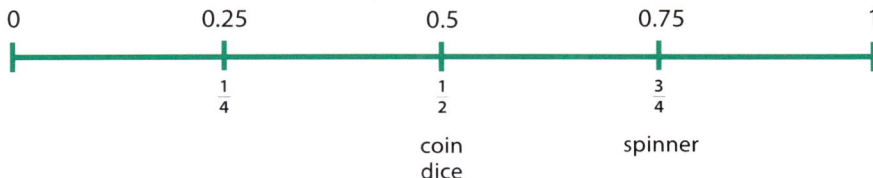

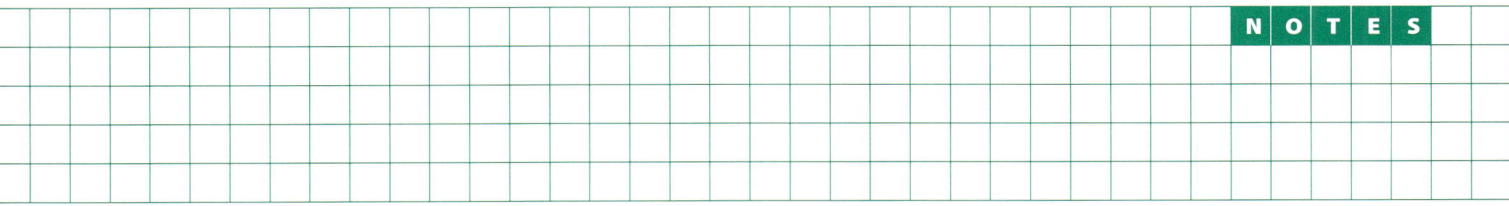

The counters

What is the probability that I will choose a white counter? There are ten counters to choose from, so there are ten possible outcomes. Three of these outcomes are white, so the probability of drawing a white counter is three out of ten or $\frac{3}{10}$. This is 0.3 as a decimal.

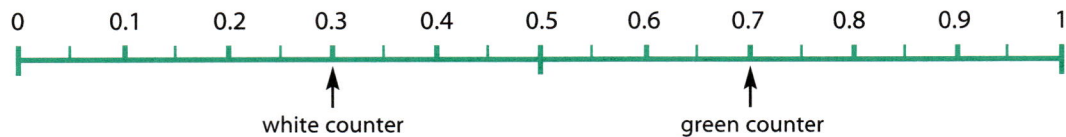

Can you see why the probability of drawing a green counter is 7 out of 10, or $\frac{7}{10}$, or 0.7?

Experimental evidence

Sometimes it is more difficult to calculate probabilities.
This is usually when they are based around data from a survey or experiment.

The cars

What is the chance that the next car down the road is red? This depends on a lot of things, such as the fashion, and the tastes of people who buy cars. The colours of the cars are not equally likely. You are more likely to see a red car than a pink one! For your road, the only way to estimate it is by doing a survey and looking at the data.

Colour	Frequency
Red	8
Blue	6
Green	4
Black	1
Pink	1

The table shows the colours of twenty cars counted down my road.

Red appears to be the most common! The chance of the next car being red is about eight in twenty or $\frac{8}{20}$.

As a decimal, this is 8 ÷ 20 = 0.4. Where does this decimal come on the line? In a similar way the probability of this next car being blue is six in twenty or $\frac{6}{20}$. As a decimal this is 0.3.

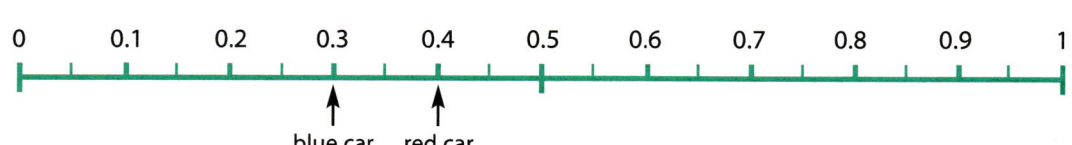

THINK ABOUT IT

If we add up all the probabilities of all the possibilities we should get 1. Try it for the examples above.

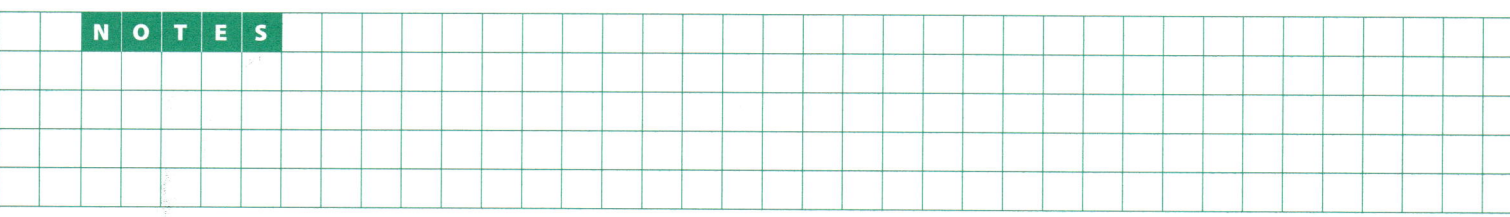

N O T E S

England winning the next World Cup

There have been sixteen World Cups and England have won only once. The experimental evidence suggests that the chance that they will win it is one in sixteen or $\frac{1}{16}$.
(In actual fact it is not really correct to estimate probabilities this way since the teams have all changed over the years. Still, it's rather a low chance whichever way you look at it!)

Where would this go on the line? Imagine the line divided up into 16 sections.

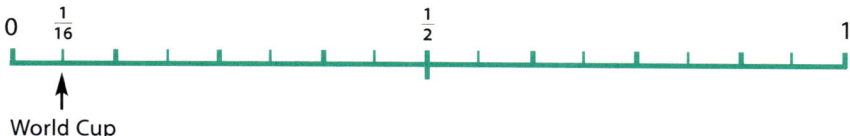

World Cup

The chance of England winning is one section along! Rather near the impossible end!
As a decimal, $\frac{1}{16} = 0.0625$.

DID YOU KNOW?
The most goals scored in an international match was by Hungary in 1982. They scored 10! Rather a rare result, don't you think!

 Comparing probabilities

We should now be able to compare the probabilities of all the events.
Look at all the probabilities we have calculated, and put them all on one line.

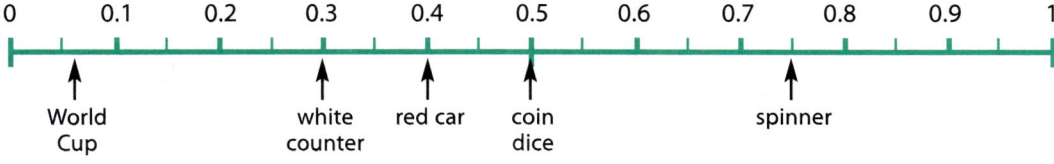

World Cup   white counter   red car   coin dice   spinner

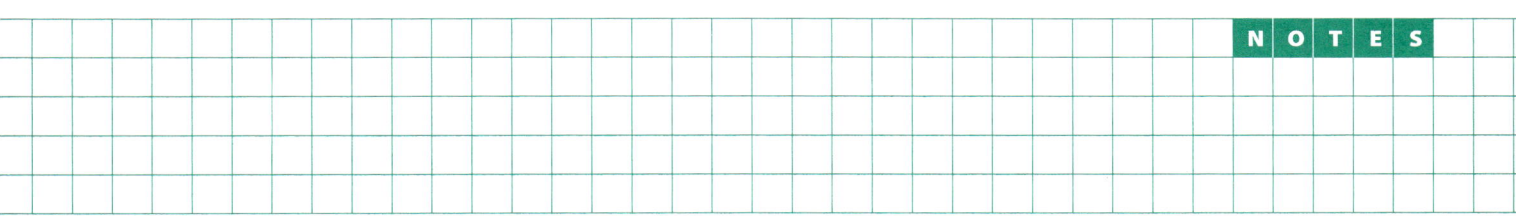

How do they compare with your estimates? The spinner landing on green was the most likely and England winning the next World Cup was the least likely.

Decimals are an excellent way to compare probabilities, as they are easier to compare than fractions, where the denominators can be different.

EXAMPLE

Which is most likely, getting a 5 on a dice or seeing a green car coming down my road?

The probability of getting a 5 on a dice is one in six or $\frac{1}{6}$.
The probability of a green car (from the previous data) is $\frac{4}{20}$.
Which fraction is biggest? Converting to decimals will make it easier.
The probability of getting a 5 on a dice is $1 \div 6 = 0.166666$, or 0.17 when rounded.

The probability of seeing a green car we have already worked out by doing $4 \div 20 = 0.2$. You can now compare the probabilities easily, because 0.2 is bigger than 0.17.

You are more likely to see a green car coming down my road than to get a 5 on a dice.

KEY CONCEPTS

❋   The probability of an event happening is all about what you expect to happen

❋   Probabilities are measured on a line, with 0 (impossible) at one end, and 1 (certain) at the other

❋   To calculate the probability of event A happening, first count up all the different things that could happen (the total number of possible outcomes). Then count up the number of ways of getting event A.

Then the probability is (ways of getting event A) in (total number of outcomes)

This can be written as a fraction as: $\frac{\text{ways of getting event A}}{\text{total outcomes}}$

❋   Compare probabilities by converting to decimals. (To convert a fraction to a decimal divide numerator by denominator.) To picture the decimal you have calculated, imagine the whole line divided up into sections, one section for each possible outcome. Then count along the sections until you get to the number of ways of getting event A

N O T E S

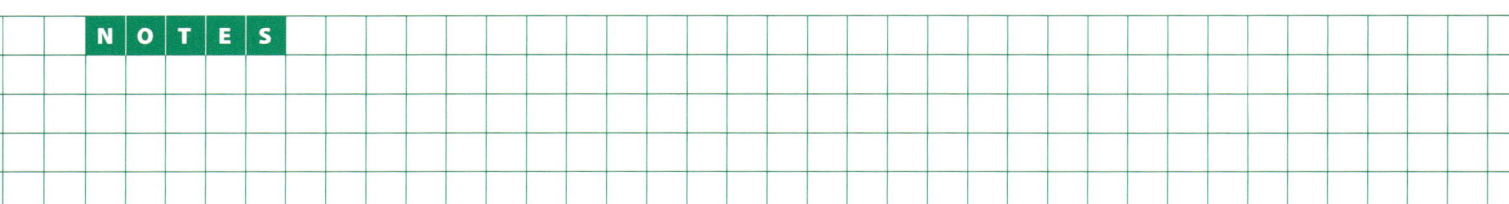

REVIEW

1. A dice is thrown. Work out the probabilities of getting:

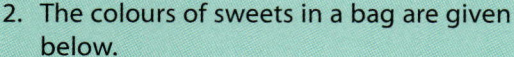

   a. a score of 2
   b. an even number
   c. a score greater than 4
   d. a score less than 1

2. The colours of sweets in a bag are given below.

Colour	Frequency
Blue	51
Yellow	39
White	10

   a. You draw one sweet from the bag. What is the probability of it being blue? Yellow? White?
   b. Show your results on a probability line.

3. In a raffle I buy five tickets. A total of two hundred are sold. What is the probability that I win?

HIGHER PERFORMANCE

1. At a fair there are two games. In Game 1 an eight sided spinner is spun. You win if you land on yellow.

   In Game 2 a counter is picked at random from a bag containing five red counters and seven blue counters. You win if you pick a red counter.

   Which game are you most likely to win? (Hint: Work out the probability of each, then convert to decimals.)

2. At a fair the spinner shown is spun 120 times. You win 10p if you land on the WIN sections. How much do you expect would be paid out in prizes?

Answers

1. Game 1: Probability of winning is $\frac{3}{8} = 0.375$
   Game 2: Probability of winning is $\frac{5}{12} = 0.417$
   You are most likely to win on Game 2.

2. £4
   The chance of winning is two in six, which is $\frac{1}{3}$. This means you expect to pay out a third of the time. One third of 120 spins is $120 \div 3 = 40$.
   Forty wins at 10p per win = £4.

Answers

1. a. $\frac{1}{6}$ b. $\frac{3}{6}$ or $\frac{1}{2}$ c. $\frac{2}{6}$ or $\frac{1}{3}$ d. $\frac{0}{6}$ or 0

2. a. Blue is fifty-one in a hundred = $\frac{51}{100} = 0.51$
   Yellow is thirty-nine in a hundred = $\frac{39}{100} = 0.39$
   White is ten in a hundred = $\frac{10}{100} = 0.1$

   b.
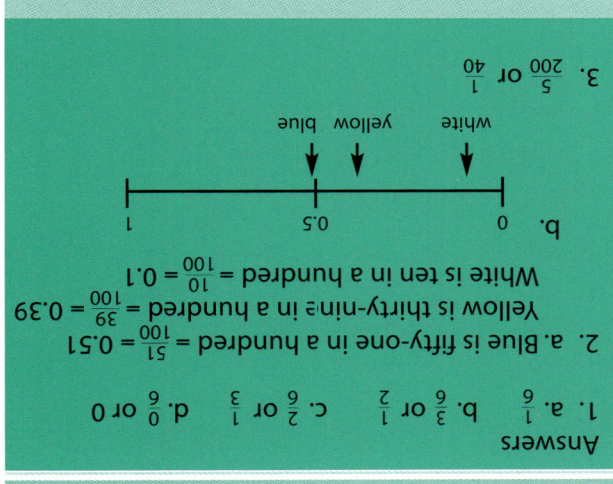

3. $\frac{5}{200}$ or $\frac{1}{40}$

| H14 | Estimating Probability using Relative Frequency | H14 |

In ▶ H13, Simple Probability, we saw that it is easy to work out probabilities by counting up all the possible outcomes. We also saw that the probability of some events cannot be calculated using theory, but only using data from a survey or experiment. When you use data in this way you are working out the relative frequency with which that event has occurred in the past. This is that same as the proportion of the time it has occurred in the past.

Let's say you did an experiment to find out the probability of event A happening:

Relative frequency of event A is   (total number of times you got event A)

in

(total number of times you did the experiment)

This can be written as a fraction easily: $\dfrac{\text{number of times you got event A}}{\text{total number of times you did the experiment}}$

EXAMPLE
In a fairground there is a game based around a spinner. If the spinner lands on the WIN section, you win a cuddly toy!

Being a clever mathematician you decide to work out whether it is worth playing or not. Using probability theory, the chance of winning is two out of five or $\frac{2}{5}$ as a fraction. Remember that this is 0.4 as a decimal.

This means that you would expect two in every five people to win the game. You watch for a while to check if this actually happens. (After all, they may have weighted the spinner so that it does not land on the WIN section at all!)

Over ten games you collect the following results:

WIN	LOSE
3	7

The relative frequency of winning is therefore three in ten.
As a fraction this is $\frac{3}{10}$. As a decimal it's 0.3.

How does this compare with what you expected? It's slightly less than you expected. Why?

N O T E S																			

There are two possible reasons. Either the spinner is weighted so that it lands on Lose more often than you would expect or you don't have enough results to give a true picture. After all, you have only looked at ten games.

You decide to look at fifty games instead to get a better estimate:

WIN	LOSE
19	31

This time, the relative frequency of winning is $\frac{19}{50}$, which is 0.38.

This seems much nearer what you expected to get using theory. Remember, things don't always work out **exactly** as expected.

It looks as if the spinner isn't weighted after all.
This means you would **expect** to win about twice in every five games.

Sometimes you cannot compare theoretical probability with experimental probability. This happens when we are considering statistical evidence.

What is the probability that it will snow in London on Christmas Day (25 December)? You may think it is fifty-fifty chance (Evens) since it may snow or may not snow. This would be wrong as it is much more likely **not** to snow than to snow.

Let's look at statistics for the twentieth century.
In the 1900s there were only nine white Christmases in London. This is a relative frequency of nine in a hundred, or 0.09.

Look back at ▶ H13, Simple Probability, where we considered the probability that the next car coming down my road would be red. We calculated the relative frequency of the car being red and it was about 0.4. If we had counted more cars we would have had a better estimate of the probability.

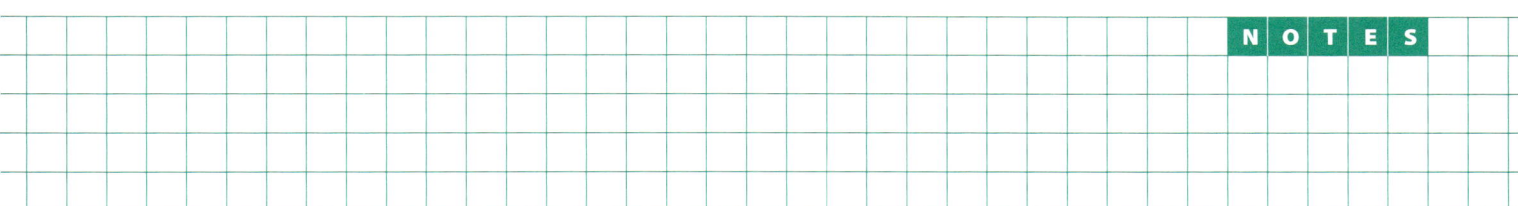

KEY CONCEPTS

There are two ways to calculate probability: theoretical and experimental ✳

Theoretical probability is calculated by counting up all possible outcomes. ✳

Probability of A = $\dfrac{\text{number of ways of getting A}}{\text{total number of outcomes}}$

Experimental probability is calculated by looking at statistical evidence and working out the relative frequency. The more data you can collect, the better the estimate of the probability ✳

Relative frequency of event A = $\dfrac{\text{number of times you got event A}}{\text{total number of times you did the experiment}}$ ✳

N O T E S

REVIEW

1. When two coins are tossed you could get two heads, or two tails or a tail and a head. You toss the two coins fifty times, and record your results in a table:

Event	Frequency
Two heads	12
Two tails	14
A head and a tail	24

Work out the relative frequency of each event. Is this what you expected?

2. A traffic survey was completed to measure the speed of cars driving past. The data were grouped together in this table.

   a. Find the mode average speed.

   b. Given that the speed limit is 30 mph, what is the probability that a car breaks the speed limit?

   c. Use the data and your answers to **a** and **b** to describe how safe the road is.

Speed of car (mph)	Frequency
1–10	2
11–20	5
21–30	16
31–40	13
41–50	4
51–60	1

Answers

1. Two heads: $\frac{12}{50}$ or 0.24
   Two tails: $\frac{14}{50}$ or 0.28
   A head and a tail: $\frac{24}{50}$ or 0.48

   Looking at the theory, there are actually four possible things that could happen. So the theoretical probabilities are:

   Two heads: $\frac{1}{4}$, or 0.25
   Two tails: $\frac{1}{4}$, or 0.25
   A head and a tail: $\frac{1}{2}$, or 0.05

Coin 1	Coin 2
H	H
T	T
H	T
T	H

   This is roughly what we got by experimenting. Doing the experiment more times would give a closer result (unless the coins were weighted).

2. a. The mode average is 21–30 mph.
   b. The number of cars driving at more than 30 mph is eighteen in forty-one.
      The relative frequency of breaking the speed limit is 18 ÷ 41 = 0.44.
   c. The mode average is under the speed limit. However, the probability that a car taken at random breaks the speed limit is 0.44, which is quite a high frequency (nearly half). The road is not very safe.

H15   Listing all Outcomes   H15

In ▶ H13, Simple Probability, and ▶ H14, Estimating Probabilities using Relative Frequencies, we have considered how to work out the probability of various events, either by counting up outcomes or by looking at statistical data. Sometimes we also need to work out the probability

EXAMPLE

In a class there are three boys, Josef, Ali and Bob, and three girls, Maya, Liz and Kamala. They are standing for the school council. A boy and a girl are picked at random from this group. What is the probability that Josef and Maya are picked?

First of all we need to list all the possible pairs that can be picked.
These are the **possible outcomes**.
Then we need to count how many of these pairs involve Josef and Maya.
Then the probability is:

(number of ways of choosing Josef and Maya) in (total number of possible pairs)

Let's list all the possible pairs. Try to be **systematic** (this means do it in a logical order).

List all the pairs with Josef first:

Josef and Maya
Josef and Liz
Josef and Kamala

Then list the pairs with Ali, and then with Bob:

Ali and Maya   Bob and Maya
Ali and Liz   Bob and Liz
Ali and Kamala   Bob and Kamala

Altogether there are nine possible pairs. One of these is Josef and Maya.
This means the probability of picking Josef and Maya is 1 out of 9 or $\frac{1}{9}$.

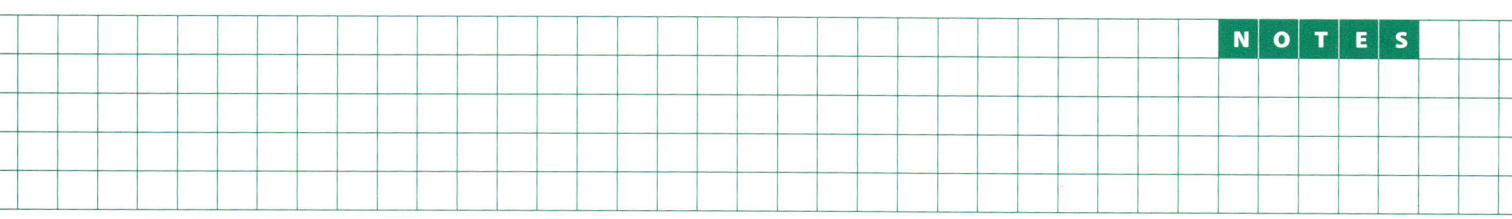

N O T E S

EXAMPLE   At a fairground a game is based around two dice. The dice are thrown at the same time. The scores shown are added together. Different scores have different amounts of prize money.

What possible totals could you have?
Which total score do you think would come up the most?
We can only find this out by listing all the outcomes.

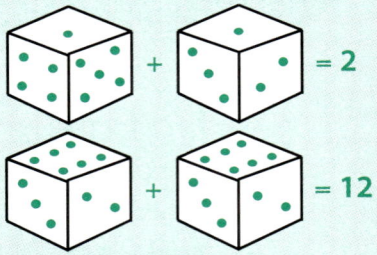

The smallest total possible must be 2, since 1 and 1 would give a total of two. The biggest total is 12 from getting a 6 and a 6.

We *could* start listing all the totals long hand, like we did before. This gets quite tedious!
To make it simpler, let's represent the event '1 on first dice and 2 on second dice' as (1, 2).
Then show all these outcomes in a **sample space diagram**:

The scores on the first dice are listed along the bottom, and the scores on the second dice up the side. Then, just like coordinates, you can read off all the possible scores from the diagram. You can see that the total score 7 comes up the most.

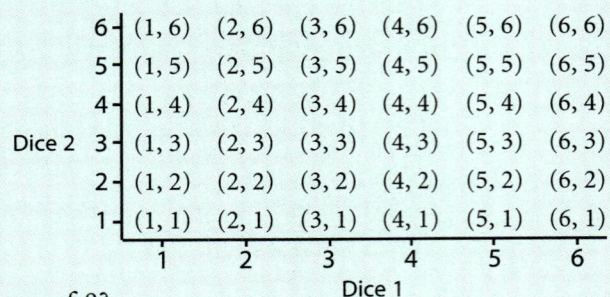

Dice 2						
6	(1, 6)	(2, 6)	(3, 6)	(4, 6)	(5, 6)	(6, 6)
5	(1, 5)	(2, 5)	(3, 5)	(4, 5)	(5, 5)	(6, 5)
4	(1, 4)	(2, 4)	(3, 4)	(4, 4)	(5, 4)	(6, 4)
3	(1, 3)	(2, 3)	(3, 3)	(4, 3)	(5, 3)	(6, 3)
2	(1, 2)	(2, 2)	(3, 2)	(4, 2)	(5, 2)	(6, 2)
1	(1, 1)	(2, 1)	(3, 1)	(4, 1)	(5, 1)	(6, 1)
	1	2	3	4	5	6

Dice 1

What is the probability that you will get a total score of 8?

From the diagram, read them off. They lie in a diagonal line!

$$(2, 6), (3, 5), (4, 4), (5, 3), (6, 2)$$

There are five possible ways of getting a total score of 8.

How many possible outcomes are there *altogether*? Again, look at the diagram. There are six rows of six, making a total of thirty-six possible outcomes. So the probability of getting a score of 8 is five in thirty-six or $\frac{5}{36}$. This total comes up a lot in the diagram, so it will get thrown quite frequently. This means it should have a low prize!

Which score would **you** give the highest prize to? It has to be the one that comes up the **least** often so that the game will make some money! Which score should be the losing score? This has to be the one that comes up the **most** often.

THINK ABOUT IT

In this game if you throw one particular total you should immediately lose! Which total do you think this is? What is the chance of getting this total? There are two totals that could win the jackpot! Which do you think these are? They should be the least likely. What is the chance of getting each of these totals?

N O T E S

Listing all outcomes using tree diagrams

There is a third way to show all outcomes which can sometimes be even simpler. This is by using a tree diagram. The diagram branches like a tree.

EXAMPLE   In a school canteen there are three choices for the main course: sausages, burger or fish.
There are two choices for pudding: ice-cream or apple pie.
List all the possible meals.

The first column of branches on the tree show the choices for main course.
The second column of branches show the choices for pudding:
In this way each column represents a new decision which has to be made.

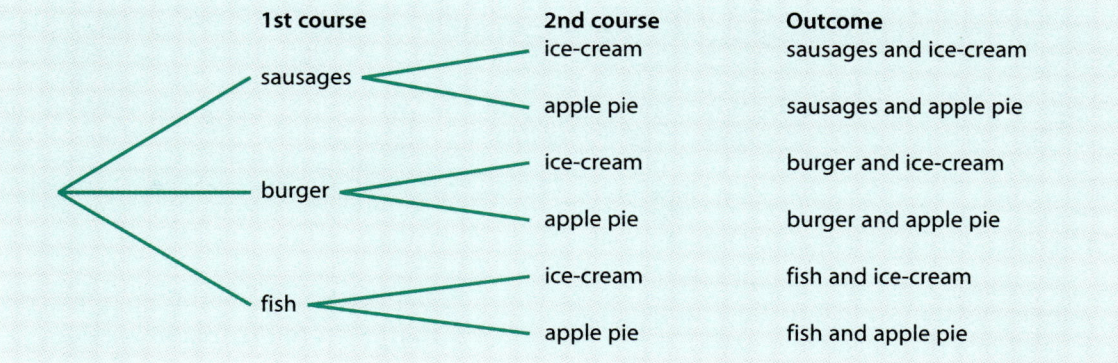

Notice two things:
- The tree is in very strict columns, one column for each decision. This helps you make sure you have listed all the possible outcomes
- Each of the puddings appears three times; once for each of the choices of first course

If all these choices are equally likely, what is the probability that someone will choose sausages and ice-cream? You can see from the diagram that there are six possible outcomes. One of these meals is sausages and ice-cream. The probability of picking this meal is therefore one in six, or $\frac{1}{6}$.

What is the probability that someone picks fish or burger with apple pie? There are two ways of doing this. The probability of this happening is $\frac{1}{3}$. As a simpler fraction this is $\frac{2}{6}$.

 ## Notation

As mathematicians we like to use shorthand wherever possible. For probabilities we write 'the probability of event A happening is x' as P(event A) = x.

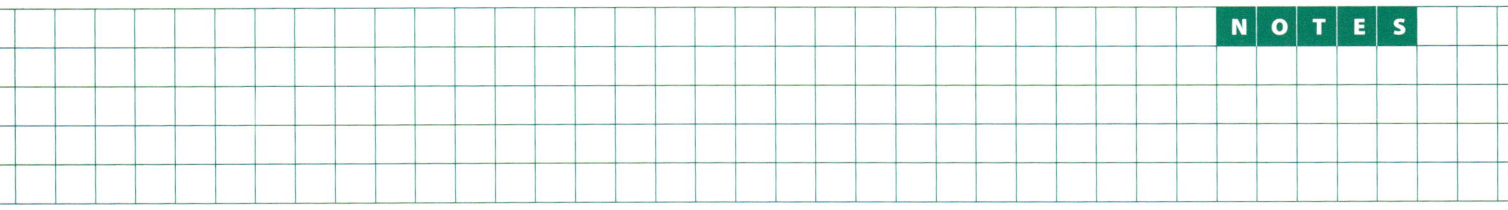

NOTES

KEY CONCEPTS

✳ When calculating probabilities involving two or more events happening together, first list all the possible things that could happen. This is called listing *all possible outcomes*

✳ This can be done in three ways: writing a long list, using a sample space diagram, or using a tree diagram. It doesn't matter which way you choose, but sometimes one way will be easier than the others

✳ Then always use the simple rule.
The probability of getting event A is (ways of getting event A) in (total number of outcomes)

$$\text{probability of getting event A} = \frac{\text{ways of getting event A}}{\text{total outcomes}}$$

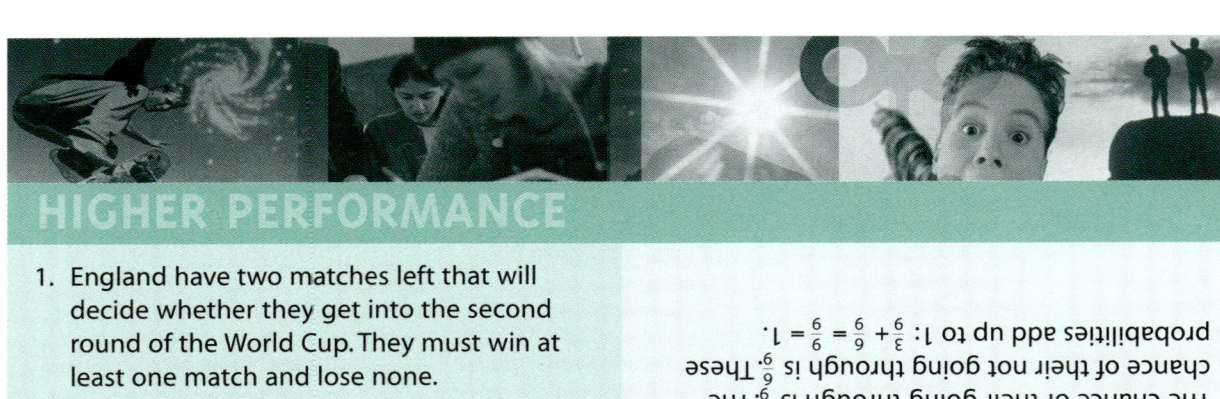

HIGHER PERFORMANCE

1. England have two matches left that will decide whether they get into the second round of the World Cup. They must win at least one match and lose none.

   a. List all the possible outcomes using a tree diagram.

   b. If each of these outcomes is equally likely, what is the probability that they will get through to the next round?

   c. What is the probability that they will not get through? How are your answers to **b** and **c** related?

Answers

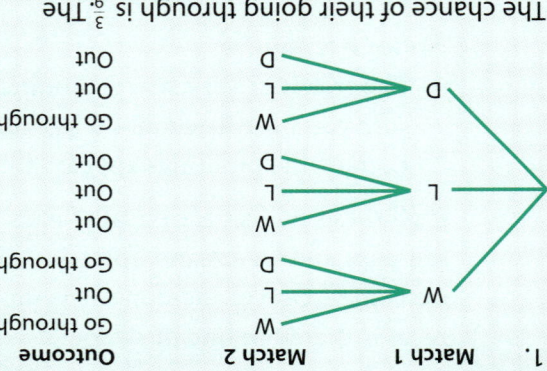

1.   Match 1   Match 2   Outcome

              W   Go through
         W   L   Out
              D   Go through
              W   Out
         L   L   Out
              D   Out
              W   Go through
         D   L   Out
              D   Out

The chance of their going through is $\frac{3}{9}$. The chance of their not going through is $\frac{6}{9}$. These probabilities add up to 1: $\frac{3}{9} + \frac{6}{9} = \frac{9}{9} = 1$.

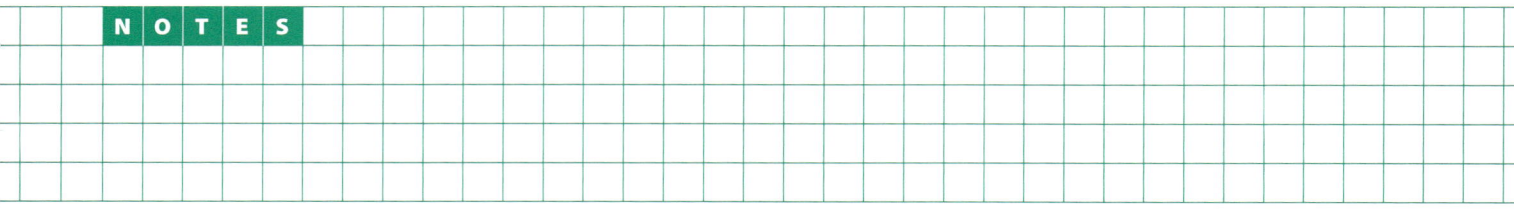

H16 · Mutually Exclusive Events · H16

For this section you need to know how to add and subtract fractions. Revise N14, Simple Addition and Subtraction of Fractions.

From now on I shall write the probability of event A happening as P(A).

In this section we will work out how to find the probability of an event *not* happening.

We will also show how to find the probability of one event *or* another event happening.

In order to do this you need to understand about mutually exclusive events. Two events are **mutually exclusive** if they cannot happen at the same time.

Which of the following pairs of events are mutually exclusive?

- Being a boy and being a girl
- Getting a 5 on a dice and not getting a 5 on a dice
- Having brown hair and having blue eyes

The first two pairs of events are mutually exclusive as they cannot happen at the same time.

The last pair are not mutually exclusive, as it is possible to have brown hair and blue eyes at the same time.

It would be easy to decide how many boys are in your class and how many girls because they fall into two distinct groups. No one would fall into both groups!

If you counted up those who had brown hair and those who had blue eyes, there would be some people who would fall into both groups. They would be counted twice. This would make it more difficult to count each group.

✳ Calculating probabilities of mutually exclusive events

If you know the probability of an event happening, what is the probability of it *not* happening? These events must be mutually exclusive: an event can either happen or not happen!

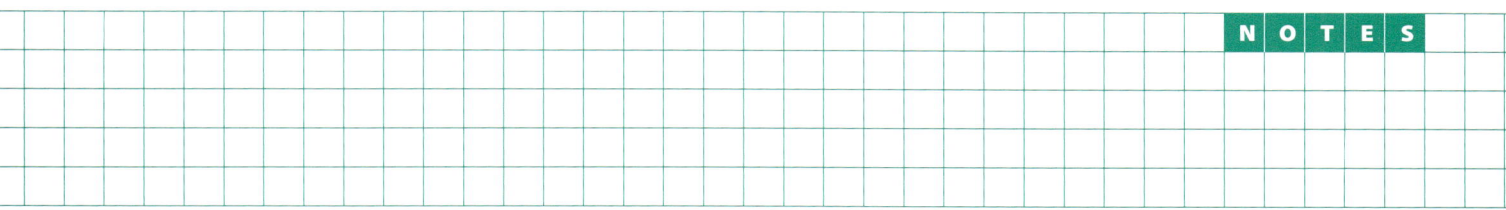

EXAMPLE In a bag of five counters, three are red. The probability of drawing a red counter at random is $\frac{3}{5}$.

The probability of not drawing a red counter is $\frac{2}{5}$, since there are two counters that are not red.

The two probabilities add up to 1. $\frac{3}{5} + \frac{2}{5} = \frac{5}{5} = 1$

If you know the probability of event A happening then you can work out the probability of it *not* happening by finding:

$$1 - P(A)$$

EXAMPLE I can either be on time for school (arrive before the bell) or I can be late.

Suppose the probability that I am on time for school is $\frac{3}{7}$. Then the probability that I am not on time (I am late) is $1 - \frac{3}{7} = \frac{4}{7}$.

This works because there are only two possible events. I can only be late or early, but not both.

EXAMPLE Remember the sample space diagram that we drew in ▶ H15, Listing all Outcomes? We listed all the possible outcomes when adding together the scores on two dice. Look at the sample space diagram on page 82.

What is the probability that I score a total of 5 or a total of 6?

There are four ways of scoring a total of 5.

There are five ways of scoring a total of 6.

There are therefore nine ways of scoring a total of 5 or 6.

The probability is therefore $\frac{9}{36}$.

We *could* have worked this out by adding the individual probabilities:

$$P(\text{total of 5}) = \frac{4}{36}$$

$$P(\text{total of 6}) = \frac{5}{36}$$

$$\text{So } P(\text{total of 5 or 6}) = \frac{4}{36} + \frac{5}{36} = \frac{9}{36}$$

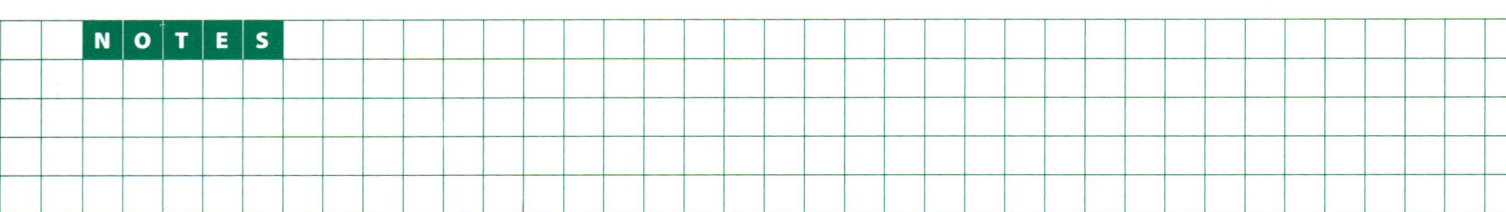

N O T E S

The 'OR' rule

For two mutually exclusive events A and B, the probability of A *or* B happening is:

$$P(A \text{ or } B) = P(A) + P(B)$$

EXAMPLE

The probability that Liverpool win their next match is $\frac{1}{2}$ and the probability that they draw is $\frac{1}{5}$. What is the probability that they lose?

Liverpool can win, lose or draw and there are no other possibilities. All three probabilities must add up to 1.

$$P(\text{win or draw}) = P(\text{win}) + P(\text{draw}) = \frac{1}{2} + \frac{1}{5} = \frac{7}{10}$$

Therefore, $P(\text{lose}) = 1 - \frac{7}{10} = \frac{3}{10}$

THINK ABOUT IT

Remember, when adding fractions they must have the same denominator. Here the common denominator is 10 since 10 is divisible by both 2 and 5.

$$\frac{1}{2} + \frac{1}{5} = \frac{5}{10} + \frac{2}{10} = \frac{7}{10}$$

Also, $1 - \frac{7}{10} = \frac{10}{10} - \frac{7}{10} = \frac{3}{10}$

Sometimes you have to be careful when using the OR rule.

EXAMPLE

In a class of thirty pupils, twenty like football and twenty-four like tennis. Work out the probability that a pupil picked at random likes football or tennis.

$$P(\text{likes football}) = \frac{20}{30} \qquad P(\text{likes tennis}) = \frac{24}{30}$$

So, using our OR rule:

$$P(\text{likes football or tennis}) = \frac{20}{30} + \frac{24}{30} = \frac{44}{30}$$

But forty-four people in thirty doesn't make sense. This gives a probability of more than 1 and all probabilities lie between 0 and 1 (recall the probability line).

What has gone wrong? Well, some pupils may have said that they liked both football and tennis. This would give an overlap between the two events. The pupils who liked both football and tennis were counted twice.

The events are not mutually exclusive because they could both happen at the same time. The OR rule works *only* if the events are mutually exclusive. Unless we know how many like both, we cannot calculate the probability that a pupil likes football or tennis.

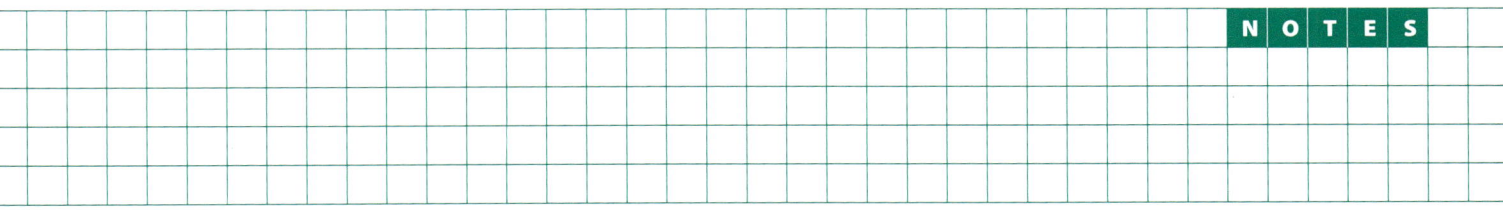

N O T E S

KEY CONCEPTS

✳ The OR rule states: for any two mutually exclusive events, A and B: P(A or B) = P(A) + P(B)

✳ The probability of event A **not** happening is calculated by: 1 − P(A)

✳ Mutually exclusive events are events that cannot happen at the same time

REVIEW

1. The probability that I pass my GCSE in mathematics is 0.9. What is the probability that I fail?

2. My pet tortoise likes lettuce, dandelions and tomatoes to eat. The probability of it eating the lettuce first is 0.1. The probability of it eating the dandelions first is 0.3. What is the probability that it will eat the tomatoes first?

Answers
1. 1 − 0.9 = 0.1
2. P(lettuce or dandelions) =
P(lettuce) + P(dandelions) =
0.1 + 0.3 = 0.4.
Therefore, P(tomatoes)
= 1 − 0.4 = 0.6

HIGHER PERFORMANCE

1. In my class there are thirty people. The tables give the numbers of people who have brown, blue or green eyes and also the size of their feet.

Eye colour	Frequency
Blue	12
Brown	15
Green	3

Shoe Size	Frequency
3	4
4	7
5	14
6	5

One person is picked at random from the class. For that person work out:

a. P(blue eyes)
b. P(size 3 feet or size 4 feet)
c. P(not having brown eyes)
d. P(feet smaller than size 6)

2. Brian says that the probability of picking someone with blue eyes or with size 4 feet is $\frac{12}{30} + \frac{7}{30} = \frac{19}{30}$. Why is he *wrong*?

Answers
1. a. $\frac{12}{30}$ b. $\frac{4}{30} + \frac{7}{30} = \frac{11}{30}$
c. P (not brown) = P(green) + P(blue) = $\frac{15}{30}$
d. P(smaller than size 6) = P(size 5 or size 4 or size 3)
You could add these separately, or just use the rule:
P(smaller than 6) = 1 − P(size 6) = 1 − $\frac{5}{30}$ = $\frac{25}{30}$
2. Brian is wrong because some pupils could have both blue eyes *and* size 4 feet. They will have been counted twice. The events are not mutually exclusive so you cannot apply the OR rule in this way.

N O T E S

H17 | Finding the Probability of Combined Events | H17

In order to understand this section, you must know how to multiply fractions (▶ N23, Simple Multiplication of Vulgar Fractions).

You should know how to use the OR rule to find the probability of one event **or** another event happening. In this section you will learn how to find the probability of one event *and* another event happening. This is called the AND Rule. For this you need to understand what independent events are.

 ## Independent events

Two events are independent if one event happening does not affect the probability of the other event happening.

Which of the following pairs of events are independent?

- Throwing a coin and rolling a dice
- Picking a girl from a class and then picking another girl
- You missing the school bus and you being late for school

The first pair of events are independent. If I throw a coin, it will not affect what I get on the dice.

The second pair of events are independent, provided the first girl picked returns to the class before the second one is picked. If she doesn't, there are fewer girls left to choose from the second time, changing the probability of picking a girl the second time.

The third pair are not independent, since if you miss the bus you will be far more likely to be late for school.

In this section we will be dealing purely with independent events.

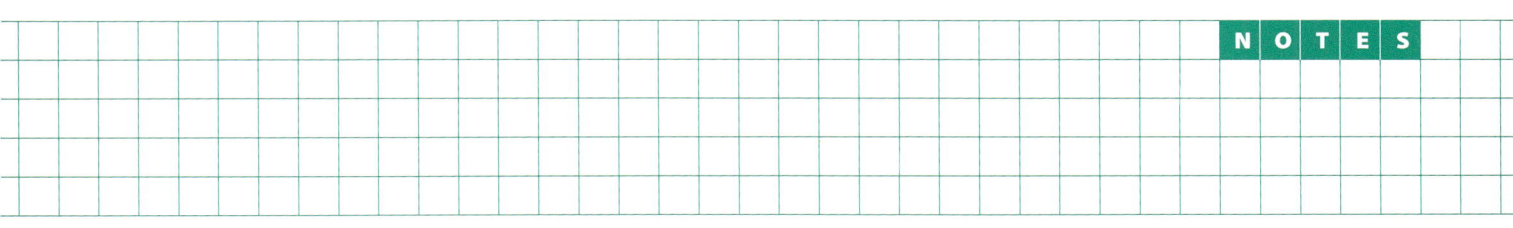

NOTES

✳ The 'AND' rule

For two independent events A and B:

$$P(A \text{ and } B) = P(A) \times P(B)$$

EXAMPLE I throw a coin and I spin a four-sided spinner. What is the probability that I get head on the coin *and* I get red on the spinner? Let's start by listing all the outcomes in a tree diagram. There are two columns, one for the coin and one for the spinner:

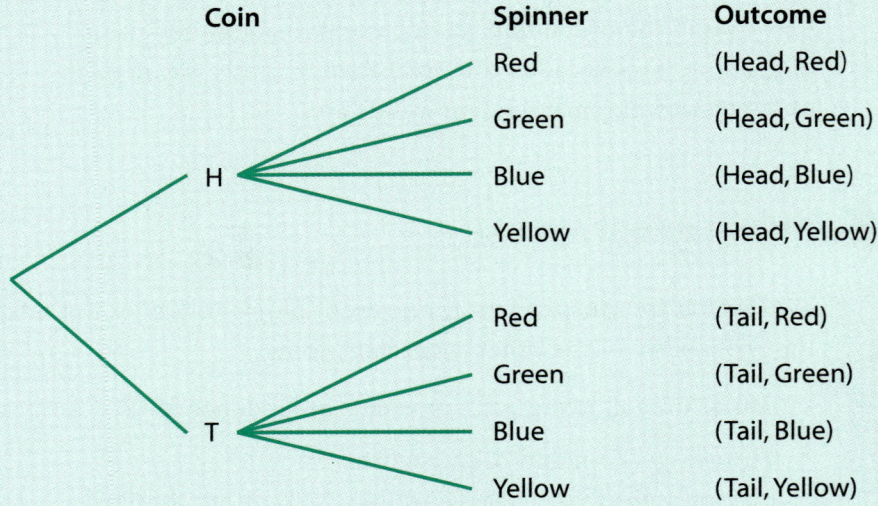

Coin	Spinner	Outcome
	Red	(Head, Red)
	Green	(Head, Green)
H	Blue	(Head, Blue)
	Yellow	(Head, Yellow)
	Red	(Tail, Red)
	Green	(Tail, Green)
T	Blue	(Tail, Blue)
	Yellow	(Tail, Yellow)

You can see there are eight possible outcomes. One of these is a head and red on the spinner. The probability is therefore $\frac{1}{8}$.

Could we have worked this out using the individual probabilities?

The probability of getting a head is $\frac{1}{2}$.

The probability of getting red on the spinner is $\frac{1}{4}$.

Look what happens when we multiply these probabilities:

$$\frac{1}{2} \times \frac{1}{4} = \frac{1}{8} = P(\text{head and red})$$

For all independent events A and B:

$$P(A \text{ and } B) = P(A) \times P(B)$$

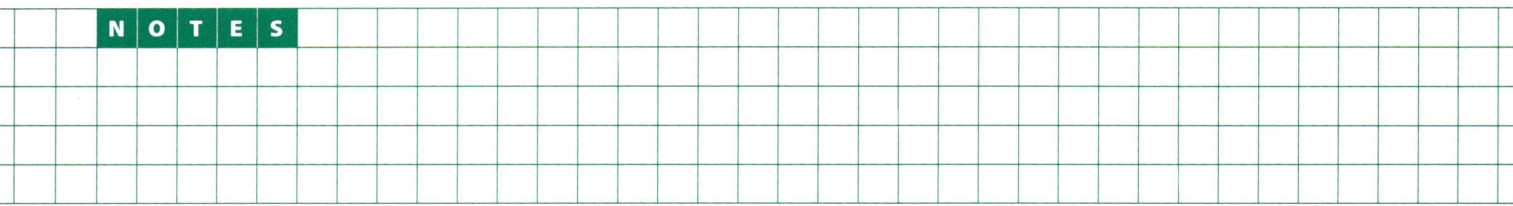

N O T E S

EXAMPLE   A fruit machine has two reels. Each reel has ten pictures. The first reel has three pictures of melons. The second reel has four pictures of melons. You win the jackpot if you get a melon on each reel. What is the probability of winning the jackpot?

P(melon on first reel) = $\frac{3}{10}$

P(melon on second reel) = $\frac{4}{10}$

P(jackpot) = P(melon on first reel AND melon on second reel) = $\frac{3}{10} \times \frac{4}{10} = \frac{12}{100} = \frac{3}{25}$

We will now combine all the theory of the last two sections to calculate some probabilities of more complicated combined events.

KEY CONCEPTS

For any independent events A and B   P(A and B) = P(A) × P(B)   ✳

For any mutually exclusive events A and B   P(A or B) = P(A) + P(B)   ✳

EXAMPLE   You are visiting the zoo in Sydney. The probability of seeing the nocturnal duck-billed platypus is only 0.1 (it is very shy). The probability of seeing the sloth is 0.4.

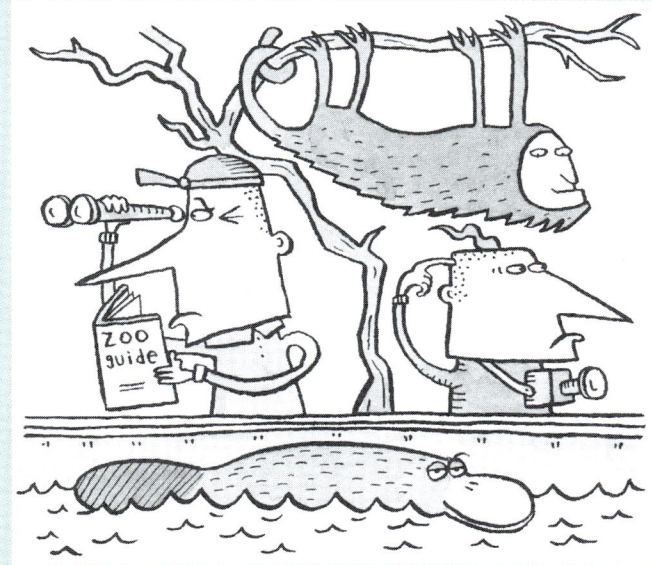

a   Draw a tree diagram to show all the possibilities of seeing these two animals

b   What is the probability of seeing the platypus and the sloth?

c   What is the probability of seeing neither?

d   What is the probability of seeing either the sloth or the platypus, but not both?

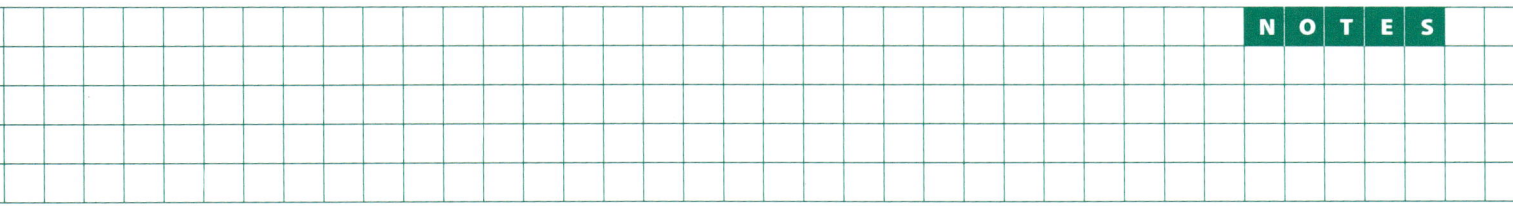

N O T E S

a First let's draw a tree diagram. This is always a good idea so that you can keep track of all the possible outcomes. There are two columns: one for the platypus and one for the sloth. There are two possibilities: either I see the animal or I don't.

To keep track of the probabilities, I will write them on the branches of the tree. Thus, P(see the platypus) = 0.1, so I write that on the first branch for the first column. P(don't see platypus) = 1 − 0.1 = 0.9. I write this on the second branch. Similarly, P(see sloth) = 0.6. So, P(don't see sloth) = 0.4.

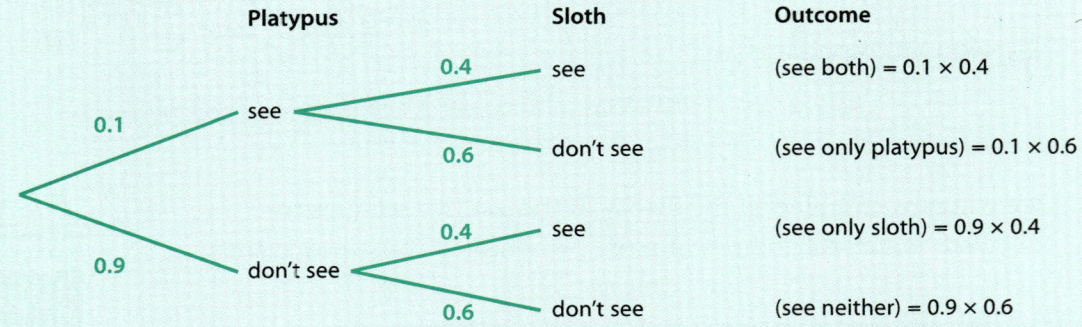

Platypus	Sloth	Outcome
	0.4 see	(see both) = 0.1 × 0.4
0.1 see	0.6 don't see	(see only platypus) = 0.1 × 0.6
0.9 don't see	0.4 see	(see only sloth) = 0.9 × 0.4
	0.6 don't see	(see neither) = 0.9 × 0.6

Now we are ready to calculate probabilities of the combined events:

b The branch labelled P(see both) gives this outcome:

$$P(\text{see platypus and sloth}) = P(\text{see platypus}) \times P(\text{see sloth})$$
$$= 0.1 \times 0.4 = 0.04$$

c The branch labelled P(see neither) gives this outcome:

$$P(\text{don't see platypus and don't see sloth}) = P(\text{don't see platypus}) \times P(\text{don't see sloth})$$
$$= 0.9 \times 0.6 = 0.54$$

d There are two branches that give this outcome. These are the ones labelled P(see only platypus) and P(see only sloth). Hence the two possible outcomes are:

$$P(\text{see platypus and don't see sloth}) = P(\text{see platypus}) \times P(\text{don't see sloth})$$
$$= 0.1 \times 0.6 = 0.06$$

or

$$P(\text{don't see platypus and see sloth}) = P(\text{don't see platypus}) \times P(\text{see sloth})$$
$$= 0.9 \times 0.4 = 0.36$$

Then

$$P(\text{see only platypus or see only sloth}) = P(\text{see only platypus}) + P(\text{see only sloth})$$
$$= 0.06 + 0.36 = 0.42$$

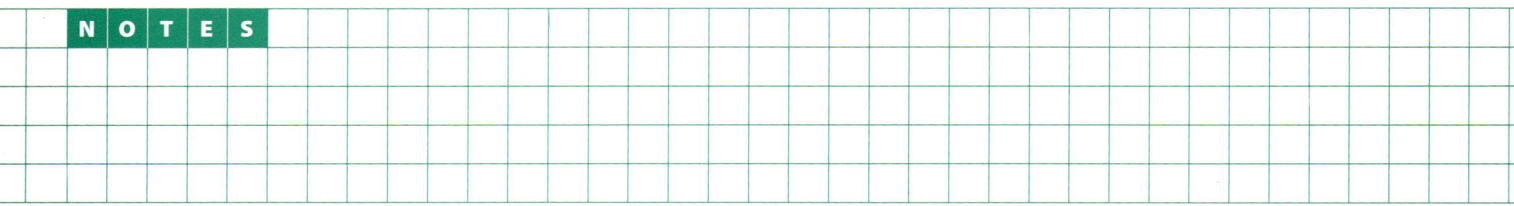

N O T E S

EXAMPLE

There are two sets of traffic lights on the road. The probability that the first set is green is 0.2. The probability that the second set is red is 0.3. Draw a tree diagram, and work out the probability that:

a You will get through without stopping

b You will be stopped by at least one of the lights

To work out the probabilities remember that the two choices at each point add up to 1. If P(G) = 0.2 then P(R) = 0.8.

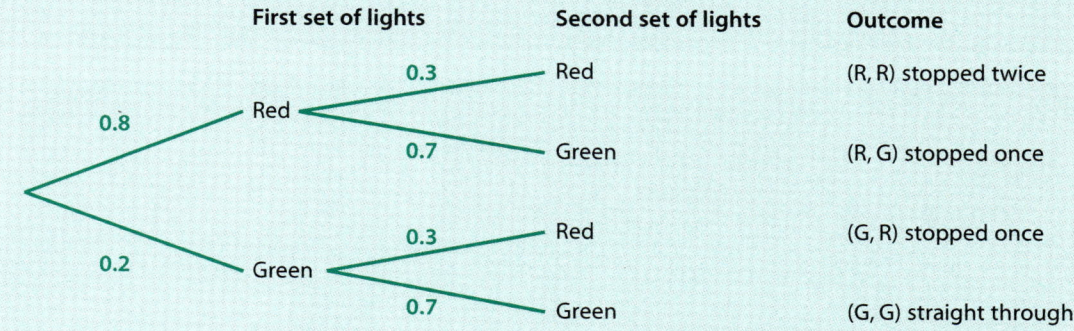

First set of lights	Second set of lights	Outcome
0.8 Red	0.3 Red	(R, R) stopped twice
	0.7 Green	(R, G) stopped once
0.2 Green	0.3 Red	(G, R) stopped once
	0.7 Green	(G, G) straight through

a P(G, G) = 0.2 × 0.7 = 0.14

b P(stop at least once); there are two ways to work this out. You can either add up the probabilities of the three paths that lead to this outcome:

$$P(\text{stop at least once}) = P(R, R) + P(R, G) + P(G, R)$$
$$= (0.8 \times 0.3) + (0.8 \times 0.7) + (0.2 \times 0.3)$$
$$= 0.24 + 0.56 + 0.06 = 0.86$$

Or you can use the fact that all the probabilities add up to 1, thus:

$$P(\text{stop at least once}) = 1 - P(\text{go straight through}) = 1 - 0.14 \text{ (from } \textbf{a})$$
$$= 1 - 0.86 \text{ as before!}$$

The second way is much quicker if you can remember to do it!

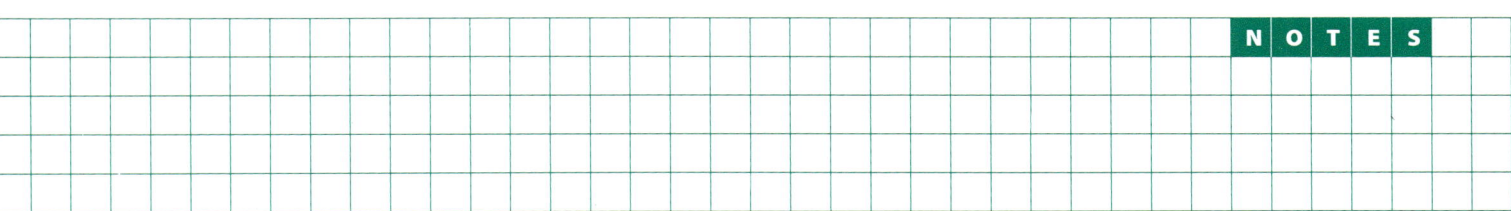

N O T E S

KEY CONCEPTS

❋ When working out probabilities of combined events follow these steps:

❋ Draw a tree diagram to identify all the outcomes

❋ Write the probabilities of each event on each branch of the tree

❋ Identify the path through the tree that gives the outcome asked for

❋ Multiply the probabilities along the path

❋ If there is more than one path that gives the outcome asked for, work out the probabilities of each path separately then add them together at the end

REVIEW

1. I pick a card from a pack of playing cards. I replace it and then pick a second card.
   What is the probability that exactly one of the cards is a heart?

Answer

1. Think of the tree diagram showing the possibilities 'pick a heart' or 'don't pick a heart' rather than all four suits. We use the notation H' for the event 'don't pick a heart'.

The probability of picking a heart is $\frac{1}{4}$ since it is one of four suits in the pack.

First card	Second card	Outcome
H $\frac{1}{4}$	H $\frac{1}{4}$	(H, H)
	H' $\frac{3}{4}$	(H, H')
H' $\frac{3}{4}$	H $\frac{1}{4}$	(H', H)
	H' $\frac{3}{4}$	(H', H')

$$P(\text{exactly one heart}) = P(H, H') + P(H', H) = \left(\frac{1}{4} \times \frac{3}{4}\right) + \left(\frac{3}{4} \times \frac{1}{4}\right) = \frac{3}{16} + \frac{3}{16} = \frac{6}{16} = \frac{3}{8}$$

N O T E S

H18   Conditional Probability   H18

The methods involved in this section are no different from the last section, except we are now dealing with events that are not independent.

If event A happening changes the probability of event B happening then we say that event B is **conditional** upon event A. The events are not independent.

EXAMPLE

In a bag there are four red balls and five green ones. I pick one out, then pick a second without replacing the first. What is the probability that I pick red first and green second?

If I pick a red ball the first time, it will affect the probability of picking a green ball the second time. The second probability is conditional on the first.
P(red the first time) = $\frac{4}{9}$, since there are four red balls and nine in total.
P(green the second time if I picked red first) = $\frac{5}{8}$, since there are five green balls to pick out of eight balls left in total.

If I picked a green first then the second probability would be different (as there would be fewer green balls to choose from).
P (green on first pick) = $\frac{5}{9}$
Then P(green on second pick if I picked green the first time) = $\frac{4}{8}$, since there are now only four green balls left to pick out of eight balls left in total.
Notice how the probabilities change depending on what you have picked the first time.

Another example is:
P(red the second time, if I picked red the first time) = $\frac{3}{8}$, since I now have only three red balls left out of eight in total.

Let's draw a tree diagram to summarise all this.

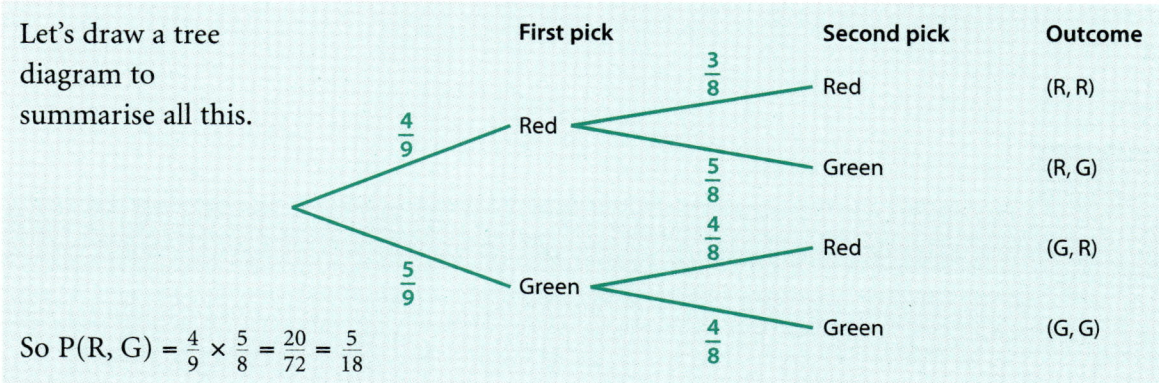

So P(R, G) = $\frac{4}{9} \times \frac{5}{8} = \frac{20}{72} = \frac{5}{18}$

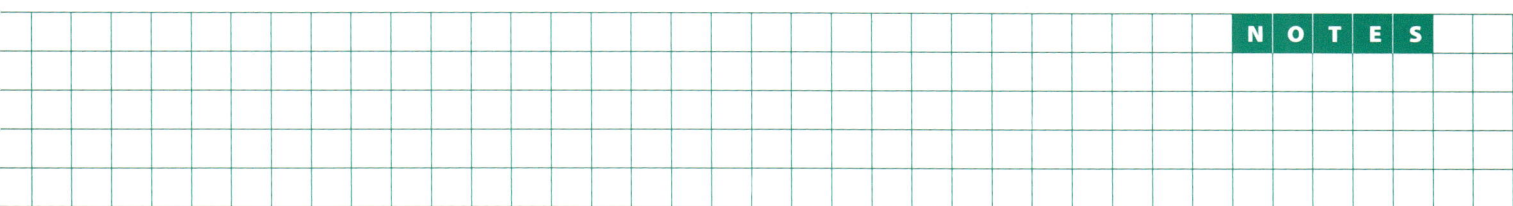

EXAMPLE

A man drives to work each morning. He has to drive past a set of traffic lights and a roundabout. The probability of the traffic lights being red is $\frac{1}{10}$.

If the lights are red, then the probability that he will have to queue at the roundabout is $\frac{3}{5}$. If the lights are not red then the traffic flows along nicely, and hence the probability that he can go around the roundabout without queuing is only $\frac{1}{3}$.

a What is the probability that the lights are red but he goes around the roundabout without queuing?

b What is the probability that he is stopped at least once on his way to work?

Draw a tree diagram, as it really helps to get all the possible routes through in order. Remember that if the event 'queue at roundabout' is Q , then the event 'don't queue' is represented by Q'.

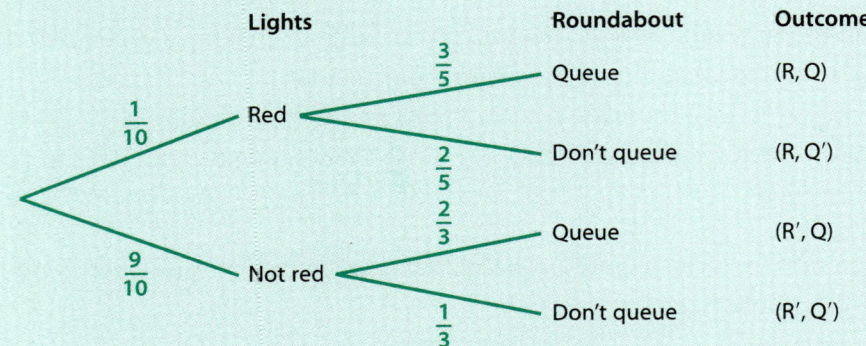

Lights	Roundabout	Outcome

a P(lights red and don't queue at roundabout) = P(R,Q')
$$= P(R) \times P(Q') = \frac{1}{10} \times \frac{2}{5} = \frac{2}{50} = \frac{1}{25}$$

b P(stops at least once $= 1 - $ P(goes straight through without stopping at all)
$$= 1 - [P(R') \times P(Q')]$$
$$= 1 - \left(\frac{9}{10} \times \frac{1}{3}\right) = 1 - \frac{9}{30} = \frac{21}{30} = \frac{7}{10}$$

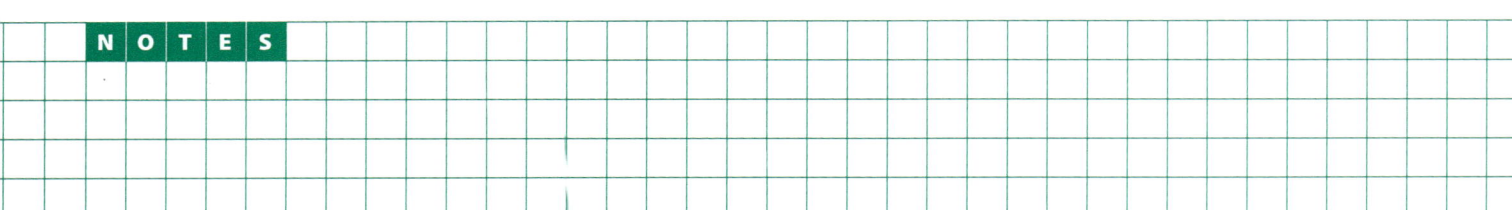

KEY CONCEPTS

✳ An event B is said to be conditional on event A if event A happening alters the probability of event B happening

✳ To calculate the probabilities, use the same methods as in H17, Finding the Probability of Combined Events. Always draw a tree diagram and remember that the probability of the second event will change depending on what happened in the first event

N	O	T	E	S

REVIEW

1. The probability of an inexperienced skier falling over and breaking his leg when it is icy is 0.2. When it is not icy, the probability is 0.05. The probability that the temperature will drop low enough for it to be icy is 0.3. What is the probability that the skier will fall and break his leg?

2. It is Tuesday. Deirdre is having a party on Saturday to celebrate her fiftieth birthday. She is having a swimming pool built for the occasion. The builders need two dry, sunny days to complete the work.

   The weather forecast says that the probability of Wednesday being wet is $\frac{1}{6}$.

   The probability that a wet day follows a wet day is $\frac{4}{5}$.

   The probability that a wet day follows a dry day is $\frac{1}{10}$.

   Find the probability that her swimming pool will be finished on time for the party.

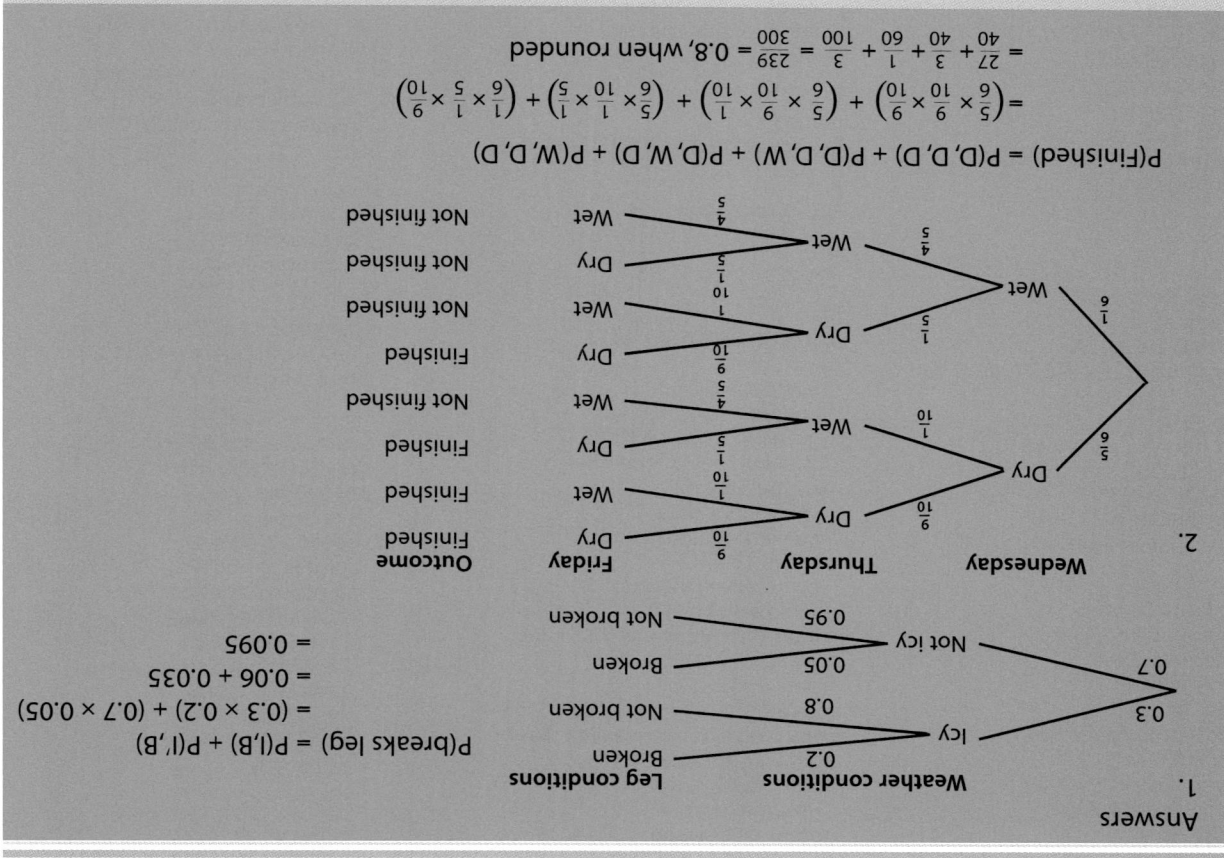

Answers

1.

P(breaks leg) = P(I,B) + P(I',B)
= (0.3 × 0.2) + (0.7 × 0.05)
= 0.06 + 0.035
= 0.095

2.

P(Finished) = P(D, D, D) + P(D, D, W) + P(D, W, D) + P(W, D, D)

$$= \left(\frac{5}{6} \times \frac{9}{10} \times \frac{9}{10}\right) + \left(\frac{5}{6} \times \frac{9}{10} \times \frac{1}{10}\right) + \left(\frac{5}{6} \times \frac{1}{10} \times \frac{9}{10}\right) + \left(\frac{1}{6} \times \frac{1}{5} \times \frac{9}{10}\right)$$

$$= \frac{27}{40} + \frac{3}{40} + \frac{1}{60} + \frac{3}{100} = \frac{239}{300} = 0.8, \text{ when rounded}$$

Index

A

age data 9
AND rule, probability 88–9
averages 10, 38–9, 41
   frequency 38–41, 43–5
   grouped data 10, 43–6, 50, 66–7
   mean 39, 41, 43, 46, 48, 63–4, 66–7, 68
   median 41, 48–51, 54
   mode 38, 41, 45, 46
   range of data 39–41
axis of graphs 18, 51

B

bar charts 16, 18, 38
bias in surveys 15

C

class intervals 10
coins, probability 71
conditionality, probability 93–4
conversion graphs 30–1
conversion of units 30–1
correlations 36
counters, probability 72
cricket, batting averages 39–40
cumulative frequency 49–50, 51, 62
cumulative frequency graph 51–3, 54
cumulative frequency table 50, 54
currency conversion 30

D

data
   collection of 6–8, 10, 13
   continuous 8–10, 19, 22
   decimal values 9
   discrete 7–8, 10, 20, 22
   grouped 7–8, 10, 22, 43–6, 50, 66–7, 68
   probability 72–3, 76–7
   range of 39–41
   standard deviation 65–6, 68
   trend line 35, 36
decimals 9, 71, 74
dice, probability 71
distance conversion 30–1

E

equivalent formula 64–5
estimates, probability 76–7
events/outcomes 79–82
   all possible 82, 84
   combined 94
   conditional probability 93–4
   independent 87, 88–9
   mutually exclusive 83–4, 89
   non-happening 84, 86
   probability 93–4
   tree diagrams 81, 82, 90–1, 93–4

F

Fahrenheit: Celsius conversion 30
formulae
   mean 68
   standard deviation 64–5, 67, 68
frequency
   averages 38–41, 43–5, 48
   bar charts 16
   histograms 19–20, 57–60
   mean 48
   pictograms 17

relative 77
tally charts 6, 7
   see also cumulative frequency
frequency chart 44–5
frequency density 60
frequency polygons 21–2

G

GCSE passes/TV watching 35
graphs 16–18, 22, 51
   see also cumulative frequency graphs;
   histograms; scatter graphs

H

height measurements 9–10, 13, 19, 21
histograms
   area of bars 57–8, 60
   continuous data 19, 22
   discrete data 20, 22
   frequency 19–20, 57–60
   frequency polygons 21–2
   height measurements 19, 21
   information from 59
hypothesis testing 12–15

I

inequalities 10
inter-quartile range 52, 53, 54, 62

K

key for pictogram 18

L

line of best fit 34, 36

M

market research 43, 46
mean 39, 41
   formula 68
   and frequency 48
   grouped data 43, 46, 66–7
   standard deviations 63–4
measurements
   continuous data 9–10
   converting units 30–1
median 48–51
   cumulative frequency 49–50, 51
   grouped data 50
   inter-quartile range 52, 53, 54
   ogive 51, 52, 54
   percentiles 51
mid-interval (middle) value 45, 66–7
miles:kilometres conversion 30–1
modal group 45, 46
mode 38, 41
   grouped data 45, 46
mutual exclusiveness 83–4, 89

N

negative correlation 36
notation for probability 81, 82

O

ogive 51, 52, 54
OR rule, probability 85, 86
outcomes: *see* events/outcomes

P

percentiles 51
   see also quartiles
pictograms 17, 18

pie charts
   angles 26, 27, 28
   mode 38
   proportion 25–6, 27
   sector 25, 28
positive correlation 36
probability
   calculating 71–2, 74
   comparing 73–4
   conditional 93–4
   data for 72–3, 76–7
   decimals 71, 74
   estimating 76–7
   experimental 72–3, 76–7
   measuring 70–2
   mutual exclusiveness 83–4, 89
   non-happening of event 84, 86
   notation 81, 82
   OR rule 85, 86
   AND rule 88–9
   theoretical 77
   tree diagrams 90–1, 93–4
   World Cup 73
   see also events/outcomes
probability line 70–1, 73–4
proportion, pie charts 25–6, 27

Q

quality sample 15
quartiles 52, 54, 62
questionnaires 14–16
questions 14, 15

R

range of data 39–41
relative frequency 77
rounding up 9, 20

S

sample space diagram 80, 82, 84
scatter graphs 33–6
sector, pie chart 25, 28
sigma 64
speed surveys 13
spinner, probability 71
standard deviation
   calculating 62–4
   data 65–6, 68
   equivalent formula 64–5
   formula 67, 68
   mean 63–4
surveys 12–13
   bias 15

T

tally chart 6–7, 10
television watching 13–14, 35
temperature conversions 30
time data 20
tree diagrams 81, 82, 90–1, 93–4
trend line 35, 36

U

units, conversion 30–1

W

weight, scatter graphs 33–4
World Cup 73